A
Vertvolta Press
REDISCOVERY
Facsimile

Vertvolta
Press

PATRONS ARE INFORMED
THAT GREAT CARE HAS BEEN EXERCISED IN
ASSEMBLING THE SPECIMENS COMPRISING
THE "DOGS OF ALL NATIONS" EXHIBIT
AND MOST OF THEM MAY BE
PURCHASED.

APPLY TO PROPRIETOR,
W. E. MASON, "DOGS OF ALL NATIONS,"
PANAMA-PACIFIC INTERNATIONAL EXPOSITION,
SAN FRANCISCO, CAL.

EUROPEAN OFFICE—
407 LORD STREET, SOUTHPORT, ENG.

DOGS

OF ALL

NATIONS

By W. E. MASON

A COMPLETE WORK, PROFUSELY ILLUSTRATED, BEARING ON
THE WORLD'S DIFFERENT VARIETIES OF THE DOG, GROUPING
UNDER THEIR SEVERAL NATIONALITIES, WITH DESCRIPTIVE
MATTER EXPLAINING THE CHARACTERISTICS AND UTILITY
OF EACH

Interior photographs are from the original 1915 edition

Book and cover design: Vladimir Verano, Vertvolta Press

print: 978-1-60944-056-5

Published in the United States by
VERTVOLTA PRESS
2614 CALIFORNIA AVE SW #236
SEATTLE, WA 98116

vvdesignpress@gmail.com
vertvoltapress.com

In Grateful Recognition

of the patronage bestowed on his effort to
assemble a representative collection
of all known breeds of dogs at

The Panama-Pacific International Exposition 1915

the author respectfully dedicates this work
to the following members of

The English Peerage

The Earl of Lonsdale, J. P., D. L.
The Earl of Huntington, D. L.
The Duke of Beaufort, A. D. C., J. P., D. L.
The Marquis of Linlithgow.
Lord Viscount Hemsley.
Lord Vivian, P. C., G. C. M. G., C. B.
Lord Middleton, J. P., C. A., R. A.
Lord Herbert Vane-Tempest, K. C. V. O.
Lord Fitzhardinge, J. P., D. L.
Sir Wm. Savory, Bart.
Sir Edmund Chaytor, Bart.
Sir Wyndham Hanmer, Bart., J. P., D. L.
Sir Daniel F. Gooch, Bart., J. P.
Sir M. Bromley-Wilson, Bart.
The Duchess of Hamilton.
Lady Viscountess Malden.
Lady Viscountess Valletort.
Lady Sophie Scott.
Lady Fairbairn.
Lady Muriel Worthington.
Lady V. Lacon.

Preface

THE world-wide and constantly increasing interest in dogs prompts the author to present in concise form, and at a price within the reach of all, a description and illustration of every variety now known to be breeding true to type.

An attempt is also made to group them in Nationalities, though, since it is admitted that the origin of certain varieties is somewhat obscure, no arbitrary lines can be laid down in this respect Originality as to descriptions is not, in many instances, claimed by the author, though where the occasion seemed to call for it, modern ideals have been incorporated in the text. On the contrary, he acknowledges with thanks the services rendered by the following accepted authorities:

Stonehenge

Count Henry A. Graaf Van Bylandt

Theo. Marples

Dr. Caius

Unless otherwise stated, the maximum sizes of the various breeds have been given. Bitches may be taken as about ten per cent. lighter than the dogs. Owing to the exigencies of space the descriptions have been confined to color, size, head, ears, eye, tail and general appearance. Dogs, all the world over, more or less, are intended to be straight and strong on the legs, possessed of well padded feet and in other ways endowed with working qualifications.

The author's object will have been attained if the subject, in the form presented, is found acceptable to dog lovers who have not the leisure to study the more exhaustive works on dogs.

English Breeds

BLOODHOUND
BULLDOG
BULLDOG (Miniature)
ENGLISH FOXHOUND
TRAIL HOUND
HARRIER
BEAGLE
COLLIE (Rough-coated)
COLLIE (Smooth-coated)
RETRIEVER (Flat-coated)
RETRIEVER (Curly-coated)
RETRIEVER (Golden)
POINTER
ENGLISH SETTER
ENGLISH SPRINGER
SUSSEX SPANIEL
CLUMBER SPANIEL
WATER SPANIEL
FIELD SPANIEL
COCKER SPANIEL

FOX TERRIER (Smooth-coated)
FOX TERRIER (Wire-haired)
ENGLISH GREYHOUND
WHIPPET
BULL TERRIER
BULL TERRIER (Miniature)
AIREDALE TERRIER
BEDLINGTON TERRIER
MANCHESTER TERRIER
MANCHESTER TERRIER (Miniature)
MASTIFF
WHITE ENGLISH TERRIER
WHITE ENGLISH TERRIER (Miniature)
OLD ENGLISH SHEEPDOG
OTTERHOUND
YORKSHIRE TERRIER
TOY SPANIEL (King Charles)
TOY SPANIEL (Prince Charles)
TOY SPANIEL (Ruby)
TOY SPANIEL (Blenheim)

BLOODHOUND

Color: Black and tan, red and tan, and tawny; the darker colors being sometimes interspersed with lighter or badger-colored hair and sometimes flecked with white. Too much white is objectionable. Height: 26 in. Weight: 90 lbs.

The Bloodhound possesses in remarkable degree every point and characteristic of those dogs which hunt together by scent. He is very powerful and stands over more ground than is usual with hounds of other breeds. The skin is thin to the touch, and extremely loose, this being more especially noticeable about the head and neck, where it hangs in deep folds. His temperament is extremely affectionate, neither quarrelsome with companions nor with other dogs, and he is somewhat shy and sensitive.

[7]

BULLDOG

Color: White or white with black mask or muzzle, brindle, red, fawns (fallows, occasionally pied and mixed colors).

Weight: A, exceeding 55 lbs.; B, exceeding 45 lbs.; C, not exceeding 45 lbs.

Until by law abolished, the Bulldog was used for bull baiting. In general appearance the bulldog should be a low-set, heavy-boned, smooth-coated dog built on broad and powerful lines. His head should be strikingly massive and large in proportion to the dog's size, the face extremely short, muzzle very broad, blunt and inclined upwards, body short and well knit, the limbs stout and muscular, hind quarters very high and strong, but rather lightly made in comparison with its heavily made foreparts. The dog conveys an impression of determination, strength and activity.

The Bulldog may be said to occupy the pride of place amongst the non-sporting varieties. Furthermore, it is one of the oldest of them and has been selected by the British themselves to typify the national character and is often termed the national breed. Certain it is that he conveys a "what we have we'll hold" impression, and for a dogged, determined, courageous and tenacious symbol one could not imagine any breed filling the role more aptly.

BULLDOG (Miniature)

Weight: Not exceeding 22 lbs.

The points and characteristics of this sub-division of the British bulldog may be summed up in the simple statement that it should be an exact duplicate in miniature of the larger specimen in every point and detail, excepting size.

[8]

ENGLISH FOXHOUND

Color: Not of great moment so long as it is not wholly black or wholly white. The favorite color is black and hare-tan, distributed in large patches on a white ground.
Height: 25 in.
Weight: 85 lbs.
A clean-cut, powerful hound. He has oblique and well laid-back shoulders, gracefully arched neck, good spring of rib, strong loins, and powerful hindquarters.
Skull should be flat, of medium width, the muzzle long, rather narrow and deep and square at the end, with large nostrils. He is endowed with extraordinary bone and hard, cat-like feet.

TRAIL HOUND

Color: White with red, brown or yellow patches.
Height: 24 in.
Weight: 46 lbs.
This is a well built and symmetrical dog with a large head, domed in skull, "stop" not too pronounced, occipital bone fairly well developed and with good length of muzzle. The eyes are rather small and brown in color. Nose sharp with open nostrils. The ears are set on low and lay close to the head. The back is strong and muscular, and chest deep. Legs straight, long and muscular. Stern is of medium length, carried higher than the back and the coat short and dense.

HARRIER

Color: Any hound color.
Height: 18 in.
Weight: 56 lbs.
The leading features of Harriers are long heads, free from "stop," square muzzles, sloping shoulders, straight forelegs, round cat-like feet, short backs, well sprung ribs, strong loins, and sound hind-quarters with well bent stifles.

BEAGLE

Color: Blue mottle, black tan and white, black and tan, lemon and white or any other hound color.
Height: 15 in.
The beagle is without doubt one of the oldest distinct breeds we have.

Beagles to be very choice can scarcely be bred too small. Although far inferior in speed to the harrier the sense of smelling is equally if not more exquisite in the beagle.

The short back, compact body, straight legs, round feet, powerful loins, nicely placed shoulders, and the true beagle head is a beautiful thing to look upon.

There are also the "pocket" beagle, which stands not more than 11 in. high and a rough or wire-haired variety, though now very scarce. They are hardy and useful in a rough country.

COLLIE
(Rough Coated)

Color: Any color is accepted provided the markings do not disfigure. The most popular colors are sable, with its many varying shades, and white markings, black with white and tan markings, and blue merles.

Height: 24 in.
Weight: 65 lbs.

The collie is a lithe, active dog, and is remarkable chiefly for his intelligent, cunning, yet kindly outlook, his magnificent coat and the devotion he displays to his master. The elegance of his outline is quite distinct from any other breed and shows great strength and activity. The head should be moderately long, proportionate to the size of the dog, with a flat skull moderately wide between the ears, and a very slight elevation at the eyebrows, and very little "stop." The muzzle should be well filled up before the eyes. The ears are small and when at attention should be carried semi-erect, with the tips turning slightly outwards. The eyes are a most important feature in this breed They should be almond-shaped, not too large or too small, set obliquely in the head, and of a dark hazel color. The blue merles should have a merled or "China" eye, though this is not an essential. On the size, color and placing of the eyes, together with the size and placement of the ears depends the expression and characteristic outlook which is so appreciated by connoisseurs. The neck should be long, body fairly short, with well sprung ribs, chest deep and forelegs straight. Any tendency to cowhocks in the hind legs should be penalized. The tail should be fairly long, carried low when in repose, and straight or gaily when excited. The coat, except on the mask, tips of ears and legs where it is smooth, should be very abundant, especially around the neck and chest, where it should form a distinct cape and frill. A dense undercoat is also very essential.

COLLIE
(Smooth Coated)

The smooth collie is identical with his rough-coated brother, excepting that the coat should be short, dense and flat, with an abundance of undercoat.

[11]

FLAT COATED RETRIEVER

Color: Rich black, free from rustiness and from white. There is also a Golden Retriever so named because of the golden or yellow color of his coat.

Height: 25 in.
Weight: 68 lbs.

The symmetry and elegance of this dog are considerable and essential, and he has a decidedly sporting character. The head should be long with the skull wide and flat at the top, and slight furrow down the middle. Eyes of medium size, dark brown or hazel in color with a bright intelligent and mild expression indicating a good temper. The neck long and muscular, chest broad and deep with well developed and well-sprung ribs. The tail should be bushy but not feathered, carried gaily but not curled over the back. His coat should be fairly long, bright, close and thick, and either straight or slightly waved.

CURLY COATED RETRIEVER

Color: Black or liver, a white patch on chest is objectionable.

Height: 26 in.
Weight: 68 lbs.

A strong, smart dog moderately low on leg, active, lively, beaming with intelligence and expression. The head should be long and narrow for the length, the eyes should be rather large and cannot be too dark. Chest not too wide but decidedly deep, back muscular and rather short with powerful loins, straight forelegs and plenty of bone. The coat should be formed of small tight curls all over the body much resembling the Astrachan.

[12]

POINTER

Color: A predominance of white is most favored by sportsmen. Liver and white, lemon and white, and black and white are also quite common. Whole colors black, liver and various shades of yellow are also quite correct.
Height: 26 in.
Weight: 70 lbs.
The Pointer is an elegantly shaped dog, symmetrical and well built all over, of great strength and endurance, yet full of refinement and very speedy. The leading essentials of a good Pointer are, pace, endurance, intelligence, and powers of smell. The head should be fairly long and broad at the skull, muzzle long and well filled up. Eyes soft and dark brown in color. Ears soft and hanging gracefully. Neck well arched and long, free from dewlap or throatiness. Ribs well arched. Loins and hind quarters very muscular. The stern must be strong at the root and free from the slightest approach to curl at the tip.

ENGLISH SETTER

Color: Black and white ticked, with large splashes and more or less marked with black, known as blue belton; orange and white, ticked as in the blacks and blues; liver and white, ticked in similar manner; black and white, with tan markings; orange or lemon with white ticks; black and white; liver and white. Pure white, black, liver and red or yellow are occasionally seen but not desirable.
Height: 24 in.
Weight: 60 lbs.
This dog owns an elegant outline. The skull is moderately narrow between the ears, with prominent occiput, a decided brow over the eyes, with long muzzle. The eyes should be dark brown in color, and are full of animation. Ears small, thin and soft, carried close to the cheeks. The neck should be slightly arched, but must not be throaty, chest deep and wide, tail should be carried with a gentle sweep downwards, and well feathered with straight silky hair. The coat is soft and silky without curl, and he should have plenty of feather on both fore and hind legs.

[13]

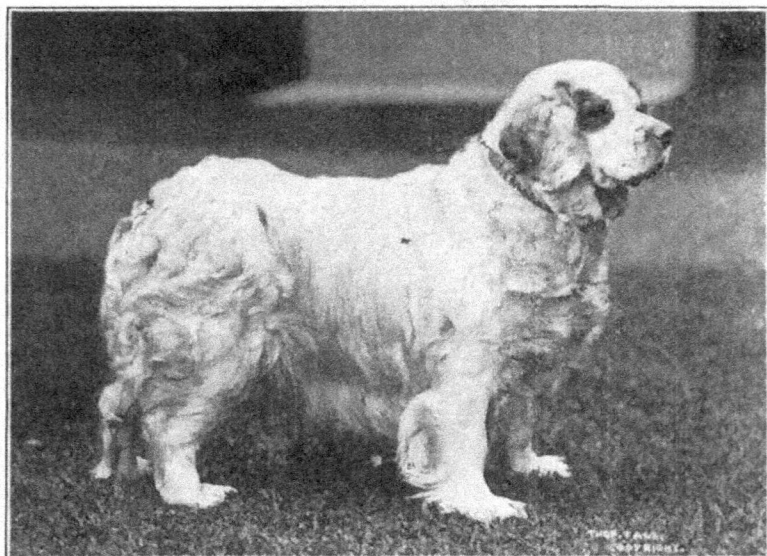

CLUMBER SPANIEL

Color: Creamy white with lemon markings; orange markings not so typical.
Height: 18 in.
Weight: 65 lbs.

This is a long, low, massive dog, with a thoughtful expression. The skull is large, massive and broad on top, with decided occiput, heavy brow and deep stop. The muzzle should be of medium length, square and with flews well developed. His orange brown eyes are of medium size and deep set. The ears are large and pointed at the tip and the hair on them should be straight. His neck is thick and powerful, well feathered underneath, and his body is long, strong and barrel-like and the hind quarters very powerful and muscular. The stern is docked, well feathered, low set, and carried level with the back, and his coat is abundant, soft and straight.

The Clumber is said to have been evolved by one of the Dukes of Newcastle at Clumber Castle, in Nottinghamshire, England, from which connection he takes his name.

The breed is also affected by other influential members of the English peerage, which, together with his dignified bearing and classical lineage, account for being dubbed the aristocrat of the spaniel family. The Clumber differs from all other varieties of the Spaniel in that he is considerably heavier and more massive and therefore less active and a slower dog in the field. For this reason he is used largely by sportsmen who do not care to travel as fast as the more agile varieties work.

Albeit as an all-round hunter the Clumber is probably without his equal and is excellent alike both as a field and water dog.

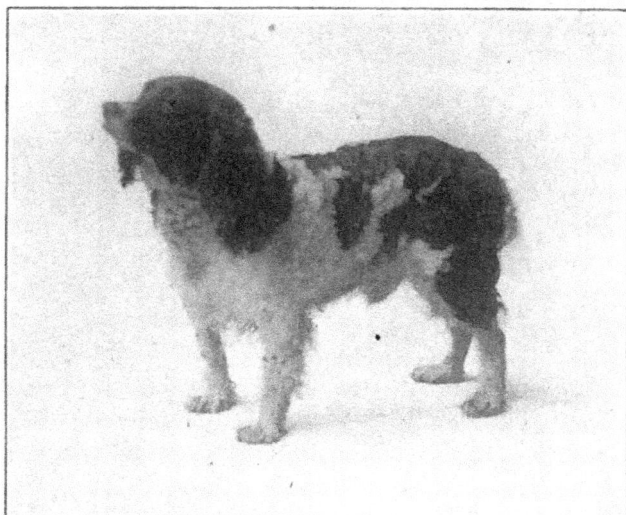

ENGLISH SPRINGER

Color: Almost any color.
Height: 20 in.   Weight: 50 lbs.

This dog is leggier in comparison to any other field spaniel and has a short and symmetrical body, long head, square muzzle, rather narrow skull, and low-set ears. He combines strength with activity, courage with docility, and all the characteristics of a workman and gentleman combined, but without his vices. The coat is thick, firm and smooth or slightly wavy, and must not be too long.

SUSSEX SPANIEL

Color: A deep shaded golden liver.
Height: 16 in.   Weight: 45 lbs.

In appearance the Sussex Spaniel is a sedate and thoughtful looking dog when at rest but is full of life and activity when at work. The skull is massive and heavy for his size with the forehead projecting over the eyes. The jaws are long and square with flews fairly well developed and nostrils large and of liver color. The eyes should be hazel in color, large and soft in expression and should not show any haw. Ears large and well furnished with silky hair. The body is long and round, with chest deep and ample. The hind quarters are very muscular. The stern should be docked to about 6 in. in length, set low, with a downward action and well feathered. A low carriage of tail is most desirable. The coat is straight or slightly wavy, thick, soft and abundant.

FIELD SPANIEL

Color: Jet black throughout, a little white on chest, though a drawback should not disqualify.

Height: 15 in.

Weight: 50 lbs.

This is a moderately low and long dog, sound in the hind limbs, with well sprung ribs and strong quarters. The head should be long and level on top, with some stop. The skull should be narrow and the muzzle deep and square. The ears are set on low and moderately long. The eye should always be dark. The coat is flat, dense and glossy, with a fair amount of feathering. Excessive feathering is objectionable.

COCKER SPANIEL

Color: Jet black. A white, short frill is not disqualified but is not desirable. Other colors—liver, lemon, red or any of these colors with white or tan or both.

Height: 12 in.

Weight: 25 lbs.

This dog should be shaped like a setter in miniature, but he is more merry and alert in expression and behavior. It is essential that he should combine small size with great activity. The skull is fairly long and forehead raised. Color of eyes varies according to the color of the coat, but should always be mild in expression. The ears are of moderate size, broad rather than long and fairly well covered with hair. His neck is long, clean, arched, and muscular, with well developed body and very strong hind quarters. The stern is docked, carried downwards, and has a perpetually vibrating movement, a sort of restless quivering, peculiar to his breed. The coat is smooth or slightly wavy, very dense but not very long.

FOX
TERRIER
(Smooth
Coated)

Color: White should predominate; brindle, red or liver markings are objectionable.
Height: 16 in.
Weight: 20 lbs.
This dog generally presents a gay, lively and active appearance. He must also possess speed and endurance, and the symmetry of an English Foxhound. He must on no account be leggy, and like a well built hunter cover plenty of ground without being long in the body. The skull is flat and moderately narrow, ears V-shaped and small, dropping forward close to the cheek, jaws strong and muscular. Eyes dark in color, small, full of fire and intelligence, neck clean and muscular without throatiness, chest deep but not broad, and the back should be short, straight and strong. His legs viewed in any direction must be straight, well boned throughout, and short and straight at the pasterns. His feet should be round and compact, tail set on rather high, always docked, and carried gaily, but not over the back or curled, and should be well coated. His coat is straight, flat, smooth, hard, dense and abundant.

FOX
TERRIER
(Wire-haired)

This variety is identical with the smooth coated Fox Terrier, except in the matter of coat, which should be broken, and the harder and more wiry the texture the better. On no account should it look or feel woolly or silky. The coat should not be too long so as to give him a shaggy appearance.

[17]

ENGLISH GREYHOUND

Color: Any color, but those preferred are black, red or brindles, fawn, blue and slates. Height: 27 in. Weight: 65 lbs.

The Greyhound's head should be fairly wide between the ears and of good length. The muzzle is long anl lean. The eyes are full, bright and penetrating, giving one the idea of high spirits and animation. The ears are set well back on the head, small and folding when at rest, but raised when in action. The neck is fairly long, arched and very flexible. The shoulders should be as oblique as possible. Chest wide and deep, back powerful and arched, loins strong, broad and deep, and the hind legs very muscular, somewhat long, the stifles strong and well bent, and very muscular thighs. The tail is long, fine and nicely curved. A terse description of this dog is contained in the following couplet:

| The head of a snake, | A back like a beam, | The tail of a rat, |
| The neck of a drake, | A side like a bream, | And the foot of a cat. |

WHIPPET

This dog is a greyhound in miniature. The weights of the racing whippet vary from 10 to 23 lbs., the best running weights being about 16 lbs., which is also considered the best size for an ideal show specimen.

BULL TERRIER

Color: Pure white.   Height: 18 in.   Weight: 60 lbs.

This is a symmetrically built dog and the embodiment of agility, grace, elegance and determination. He is styled by some as the Gladiator of the canine race. Certainly he is plucky, yet generations of training have made him the easiest of dogs to control. The skull is flat and wide between the ears, and there should be no stop. The jaws are long and very powerful, eyes small, very black and of almond shape. Ears when not cropped should be small and carried semi-erect. The neck is long and slightly arched without any loose skin. Chest wide and deep with well-sprung ribs, back short and muscular, tail short, set on very low down, thick at the root, and tapering to a fine point, and must never be carried over the back. The coat is short, close and stiff to the touch, with a fine gloss.

TOY BULL TERRIER

This dog should resemble the bull terrier in every respect except as to size. Height, 12 in. Weight, 15 lbs.

[19]

AIREDALE TERRIER

Color: The head and ears, with the exception of dark markings on each side of skull, should be rich tan, as also should be the legs to the thighs and elbows. The body should be black or dark grizzle.

Height: About 24 in.

Weight: About 50 lbs.

This dog is of a fairly recent creation. He is a sensible and companionable dog, game to the core and a fine guard. He has a well knit frame, great bone for his size, a long punishing jaw and lean head, with a keen expression and a wiry, weather resisting coat. His ears should be small and V-shaped. The tail is set on high and carried gaily, but not curled over the back. The coat is hard and wiry but not so long as to appear ragged. It should be straight and close.

BEDLINGTON TERRIER

Color: Dark blue, blue and tan, liver, liver and tan, sandy, sandy and tan.

Height: 16 in.

Weight: 24 lbs.

In general appearance the Bedlington is a lightly built, lathy dog, but not shelly. The skull is narrow, deep and rounded, high at the occiput, covered with a nice silky tuft or topknot. His muzzle must be long and tapering. The eyes are small, placed obliquely, and close together, and in shade should follow the color of the dog. The ears are moderately large, placed low, thinly covered and tipped with fine silky hair, and filbert shaped. The neck is long and chest deep, though not wide. The back should be slightly arched, and the body well ribbed up. The tail is thick at the root and scimitar shaped. The coat is a mixture of hard and soft hair, of the stand-off variety, and crisp to the touch.

MANCHESTER TERRIER

Color: Jet black and rich mahogany tan. The position of the tan markings is important. The muzzle should be tanned to the nose. A bright spot on each cheek and above each eye and the under-jaw and throat are tanned with a distinct black V mark immediately under the jaw. The fore legs should be tanned up to the knee, with black lines up each toe, and a black "thumb" mark above the foot. The insides of the hind legs tanned, but divided with black at the hock joint. The under part of the tail is also tanned, and there should be a light tan mark at each side of the chest. Tan outside of hind legs, commonly called "breeching," is a serious defect, and in all cases the black should not run into the tan, or vice versa. The two colors should be well defined.

Height: 17 in.

Weight: 20 lbs.

This is a good boned dog with the appearance of speed and activity rather than of strength, and he should be free of any approach to the whippet type. Head should be long, flat and narrow at skull, level and wedge-shaped, and well filled up before the eyes, which should be small, brilliant and dark. The ears if cropped should be carried erect. Chest narrow and deep, body moderately short with well sprung ribs. The tail is rather short and should not be carried higher than the back, and the coat is close, smooth, short and glossy.

In the opinion of many the ban of the English Kennel Club, which now prohibits the cropping of dogs' ears, has seriously impaired the popularity of this breed, as it is claimed that drop ears, no matter how small and neatly they may be carried, compare unfavorably with the smart appearance conveyed by neatly cropped ears. None the less a tremendous amount of suffering unquestionably has been prevented as a result of the English Kennel Club's ruling, and all good sportsmen will endorse its decision.

TOY MANCHESTER TERRIER

This dog should resemble his larger brother in every respect except that he should be under ten inches in height and under six pounds in weight.

MASTIFF

Color: Apricot or silver fawn or dark fawn brindle. In any case the muzzle, ears and nose should be black, with black shadings around the orbits extending upwards between them.

Height: 28 in.

Weight: 170 lbs.

This is a large, massive, powerful dog, with symmetrical and well knit frame, a combination of grandeur, good nature, courage and docility. The head offers a square appearance when viewed from any point. Great depth is much desired. The skull is broad between the ears, with muscles on the temples and cheeks well developed. There should be a depression up the center of the forehead. The muzzle is short, blunt and square. The eyes are small, wide apart, with stop between the eyes well marked, and of a hazel-brown color, showing no haw. The ears are small, thin, set on high any lay flat to the cheeks. The chest is wide and deep and the back wide and muscular with great depth of flanks. His tail is thick at the root and hangs straight in repose. The coat is short and close laying.

The Mastiff is one of the very oldest breeds known to the British Isles. The Assyrian kings possessed a large dog of decided Mastiff type and used it for lion hunting. Credible authorities point to a similarity, also, between the Mastiff and the fierce Molorsian of the ancient Greeks, and it is claimed by many students that the breed was introduced into Britain in the sixth century B. C. by adventurous Phoenician traders.

WHITE ENGLISH TERRIER

Color: Pure white.

This terrier should resemble the Manchester terrier illustrated on previous page in every respect excepting in regard to color, which should be a pure white.

OLD ENGLISH SHEEPDOG

Color: Any shade of gray, grizzle or blue with or without white markings.
Height: 24 in.
Weight: 65 lbs.

This is a strong, compact dog, profusely coated, with a characteristic ambling when trotting, and owns a thick-set, muscular short body, liberal bone, and a most intelligent expression. The skull is capacious, squarely formed, and well covered with hair. The eyes vary in color according to the shade of the dog. A "wall" or "China" eye is considered typical. The small ears are carried flat to the side of his head. Many are bred tailless, if otherwise they are docked close. The coat is profuse, of good hard texture, not straight, but shaggy, yet free from curl. He should have plenty of undercoat.

This breed is also of very early origin and has been bred in England for some hundreds of years. He is probably a relic of the early pastoral days when the wolf inhabited the British Isles, from which the flocks and herds had to be protected. Some authorities claim, however, that he is a descendant of the Russian Owtchar.

WHITE ENGLISH TOY TERRIER

This Toy Terrier should resemble the white English Terrier mentioned on previous page in every respect except as regards size, which should be under ten inches high and under 6 lbs. weight.

OTTERHOUND

Color: Grizzle and tan, blue and tan, yellow or red.
Height: 26 in.
Weight: 90 lbs.

The Rough-Coated Otterhound's head should be large, but not showing quite the peak of the bloodhound, long with strong and powerful jaws, the whole appearance being sedate and intelligent. The eye should be dark, the haw sometimes showing, but this is not a defect of the breed. His long and pendulous ears are set on close to the head and covered with hair short and fine in texture. The coat is hard, crisp, and not too long, having also a close, woolly, water-resisting undercoat.

YORKSHIRE TERRIER

Color: On the head a beautiful golden tan, much darker on the ears. The back and tail should be dark blue inclining to silver, the latter color extending over the other portions of the body, excepting the legs, which should be a golden tan.

There are two classes for weight, under 5 lbs., and over 5 lbs. but not exceeding 12 lbs.

This is a long coated pet dog, the coat hanging quite straight and evenly down each side with a parting extending from the nose to the end of the tail. His general appearance is one of compactness and neatness, with a sprightly and important bearing. The head is rather small and should be flat. The hair should be very long on his muzzle and chin, of a rich tan shade, and on no account intermingled with dark or sooty hair. The ears when cropped are carried quite erect; when not cropped, semi-erect. His body is very compact, and level on back. The tail is cut to a medium length and should be well covered with dark blue hair, especially at the end. The coat should be as long as possible, straight and glossy as silk, and not wavy or woolly.

TOY SPANIEL

Weight: Not exceeding 10 lbs.

The color of this dog varies with his breed, there being four varieties: A. The King Charles; B. Tri-color, or Prince Charles; C. Ruby; D. Blenheim.

The King Charles is a rich glossy black, with deep tan spots over the eyes and on the cheeks.

The Tri-color or Prince Charles should have the tan of the King Charles with markings like the Blenheim in black instead of red, on a pearly white ground, the ears . and under the tail should be lined with tan, and he has no "spot."

The Ruby is a rich chestnut red and a few white hairs intermixed on his chest carries great weight against him, as they do on the chest of the King Charles.

The Blenheim must on no account be whole colored, but should have a ground of pure pearly white, with bright, rich chestnut or Ruby markings, evenly distributed in large patches, and should have a spot on the forehead.

Strictly speaking this breed might, with some justice, be classed with the Spanish breeds, as unquestionably the King Charles Spaniel originally hailed from that country, but since the early part of the seventeenth century certain families of the English nobility have affected him and it is equally true to assign the production of the other three varieties to their influence and breeding operations.

The King Charles's compactness of shape almost rivals that of the Pug. He has a broad back and wide chest. The head is well domed, and in good specimens is semi-globular, and the skull should project over the eyes, so as to nearly meet the upturned nose. The eyes are se. wide apart, are large and dark, with enormous pupils. The stop is well marked, some good specimens exhibiting a hollow. The nose is short and well turned up and should be both deep and wide with open nostrils. The ears must be long so as to almost touch the ground, are set low on the head, and be heavily feathered. The coat is long, silky, soft and wavy, but not curly. In the Blenheim there should be a profuse mane. The feathering should be well displayed on the ears and feet, and on the King Charles the feathering is very long and profuse. The feathering on the tail (which is cut to the length of three or four inches) should be silky, forming a marked "flag" of a square shape, and must not be carried above the level of the back.

Irish Breeds

IRISH WOLFHOUND   KERRY BEAGLE
IRISH TERRIER   IRISH SETTER
      IRISH WATER SPANIEL

IRISH WOLFHOUND

Color: Gray, red, black, pure white, fawn and brindle.
Height: 35 in.
Weight: 150 lbs.

This dog though not as heavy and massive as the Great Dane is more so than the Deerhound. He has a commanding appearance and is very muscular, strongly though gracefully built, with movements easy and active. The head is long, skull not too broad, and muzzle moderately pointed. Eyes dark in color, ears small and of the greyhound type, neck very strong, muscular and well arched, with a long back and muscular thighs. The tail is long and slightly curved and well covered with hair. Coat should be rough and hard on the body, legs and head, and especially long and wiry over the eyes and under the jaw.

This breed is undoubtedly of great antiquity and was freely bred and used hundreds of years ago in Ireland for the hunting of wolves. When wolves became extinct the breeding of Irish Wolfhounds came to its lowest ebb, but during the last twenty years great strides have been made to resuscitate, and it is now one of the most popular of the large varieties on the show bench.

IRISH TERRIER

Color: Whole colored bright red, red, wheaten or yellow red. A little white is permissible on chest and feet, but is not desirable.

Height: 18 in.

Weight: 24 lbs.

The outstanding feature of this dog is a style of physiognomy and expression peculiarly his own. The head is a little longer than the fox terrier's, his eyes hazel rather than very dark, and so set as to give him the sort of daredevil expression for which he is so famous. The ears are small and V-shaped and drop forward close to the cheeek. The back should be strong, with loins broad and powerful. The stern is generally docked, should be well covered with rough hair but free from feathering. The coat is hard, wiry, straight and flat.

KERRY BEAGLE

Color: Black and tan, blue mottled and tan, black tan and white, tan and white.

Height: 22 in.

Weight: 45 lbs.

A well built and muscular dog. Head of moderate length, broad in skull, slightly arched from eyes to point of nose, with long round muzzle. The eyes are large, bright and intelligent, varying in color from bright yellow to a deep brown. Ears large, pendulous, falling below the neck and set on low. Chest deep but not broad. Back strong, moderate in length and muscular. The stern is long and evenly furnished with hair, thick at the root and carried curved upwards. The coat is hard, close and smooth.

IRISH SETTER

In the leading essentials, this dog is similar to its English brother, the main difference between the two is that the head of the Irish dog is not quite so long in proportion and the occipital bone not so well developed. His eyes, too, are lighter, and show less haw, and his expression, like that of the Irish Water Spaniel and the Irish Terrier, is different to any English variety. In fact it is a characteristic purely Irish expression.

IRISH SPANIEL WATER

Color: A pure deep liver without any white.

Height: 23 in.

Weight: 60 lbs.

This is a highly intelligent dog with a rare combination of power and activity. The skull is capacious with forehead prominent. Ears are set on low, are long and well feathered. The neck muscular, body well ribbed, chest deep and broad. The stern is thick at the root, is short and tapers to a fine point, and is carried quite stiff and straight. It should be covered with short, smooth hair, and present a whip-like appearance. The coat is oily and on the body composed of small crisp ringlets, on the head is a pronounced top-knot of long ringlets. The mask is perfectly smooth.

Scottish Breeds

SKYE TERRIER (prick-eared)
SKYE TERRIER (drop-eared)
WEST HIGHLAND WHITE TERRIER
SCOTTISH TERRIER
SCOTTISH DEERHOUND

GORDON SETTER
DANDIE DINMONT
CAIRN TERRIER
SHETLAND SHEEPDOG
BEARDED COLLIE

SKYE TERRIER
(Prick-eared)

Color: Dark or light blue or gray, or fawn with black points. Ears much darker than the body. Height: 9 in. Weight: 18 lbs. This is a dog of long and low structure. The skull is wide at front of brow, narrows between the ears and tapers gradually toward the muzzle. The eyes should be hazel color and set close together. Ears small, carried nearly erect, and the neck long. The back should be level and slightly declining from hip to shoulders, and should be very long and low. The tail should hang perpendicular with a slight backward curl at the end. This dog's coat should be long, hard, straight and flat, with a short, dense woolly undercoat. The hair on the head is shorter and softer than on the rest of the body, and should veil the forehead and eyes.

SKYE TERRIER (Drop-eared)

The drop-eared Skye Terrier is identical with his prick-eared brother in every respect, except that the ears are a little larger, should hang straight down, lying flat at the side of the head, and incline a little towards the front.

WEST HIGHLAND WHITE TERRIER

Color: Pure white.
Height: 12 in.
Weight: 17 lbs.

In general appearance this dog is a small, game, hardy-looking terrier, with a varminty appearance, strongly built, with straight back on muscular legs. The coat should be about two and one-half inches long, of a hard texture, with plenty of undercoat, and no tendency to wave or curl. The tail should be straight, carried not too gaily, covered with hard hair, but not bushy. The ears are small and as pointed as possible, and carried absolutely erect. Eyes of moderate size, dark hazel in color, widely placed, with a sharp, bright, intelligent expression. The muzzle should be long and powerful.

SCOTTISH TERRIER

Color: Steel or Iron-gray, Black-brindle, Brown-brindle, Gray brindle, Grizzled, Black, Sandy and Wheaten.
(White markings are objectionable.)
Height: 12 in.
Weight: 20 lbs.

In general appearance this dog should appear to be higher on the leg than he really is. He should look compact be possessed of great muscle in the hind quarters, and be powerfully put together throughout. He should own a sharp, bright, and active expression, and head should be carried well up. Skull should be long, slightly domed, very powerful muzzle and very little stop. Eyes of dark hazel color, set wide apart, small, piercing and very bright. Ears small and erect, and sharp pointed, and covered with a velvety hair. The neck is short, thick and muscular. Chest broad, body short and well ribbed up, and exceedingly strong in hind quarters. The tail is never docked and should be carried gaily. The coat is about two inches long on the body, dense, hard and wiry in texture.

DEERHOUND

Color: Dark blue-gray, brindles, yellow and sandy, red or red-fawn, especially if with black points. White is objectionable.   Height: 30 in.   Weight: 100 lbs.

In general form the deerhound should be like a greyhound, but heavier and wiry coated. The head is long and the muzzle tapers decidedly toward the nose. The skull should be flat with no stop. The eyes are dark brown or hazel, and convey a soft look in repose, but a keen far-away expression when the dog is aroused. The ears are set on high and should fall back. A prick ear is bad, and a thick ear hanging flat to the head or heavily coated is an even worse fault. The neck is fairly long and very strong, and should carry sufficient coat to form a mane. The chest is deep rather than broad, and the tail is fairly long and carried straight down or curved when in repose. The coat on the body, neck and quarters should be harsh and wiry, and about three or four inches long. The Deerhound should be a shaggy dog. A woolly coat is bad.

SHETLAND SHEEPDOG

This variety is of recent origin, the questionable intention being to evolve a toy collie. The weights aimed at are from 7 to 10 lbs., and the colors and conformation throughout should follow the collie as nearly as possible. Considerable strides have already been made in this direction, though the author does not regard the nature and disposition of a collie as suitable for lap-dog purposes.

DANDIE DINMONT

Color: Pepper or mustard. The peppers range from a dark bluish-black to a light silvery-gray. The mustards vary from a reddish-brown to a pale fawn, the head being a creamy-white.

Height: 10 in. Weight: 18 lbs.

This is a terrier of considerable antiquity. He is very game and a dog of exceptional power and pluck, yet endowed with an abundance of common sense and docility. He should be round in skull, full in eye, which should be a rich dark hazel. This dog should be strong in jaw, with short, stout legs, and long weasel-shaped body, with a soft linty coat and top-knot. A point strongly demanded is the size and carriage of his ears, which should be almond-shaped, set on low, smooth coated, with edges fringed with longer hair, and lay very close to the head.

CAIRN TERRIER

Color: The most appreciated colors are rich red-brindle and silver-gray brindle. Black mask and muzzle very desirable.

Height: 10 in. Weight: About 12 lbs.

This smart terrier is today one of the most popular of all the terrier varieties. The head is fairly capacious for his size, ears are small and carried erect, eye small, dark and of the peculiar keen "cairn" expression not found in any other breed; well sprung in ribs, abundance of bone and straight fore legs. The coat should be harsh and as dense as possible.

[32]

GORDON SETTER

Color: Red and black, with rich dark mahogany markings. The tan should appear on lips, cheeks, throat, spots over the eyes, underside of ears, front of chest, and the lower part of both fore and hind legs.

Height: 25 in.
Weight: 70 lbs.

In general appearance this is a well built and elegant dog, heavier than the English setter. His head too is much heavier in construction. The occiput is well developed, eyes lustrous, intelligent and full, ears set on low and close to the upper neck. Neck should be fairly long and not throaty, tail rather short and scimitar-like and nicely feathered. The coat is straight or slightly waved, not curly and not so fine as that of the English Setter.

BEARDED COLLIE

The points of the Highland or Bearded Collie are identical with the Old English Sheep dog except that he has a tail of moderate length and which is carried low.

He is famous as a worker of sheep and cattle and is endowed with great intelligence and highly prized in both the highlands and lowlands of Scotland, equally for his companionship and faithful service as a guard to either homestead or flock.

[33]

Welsh Breeds

WELSH TERRIER
SEALYHAM TERRIER

WELSH SPRINGER
WELSH HOUND

WELSH TERRIER

Color: Black and tan or black-grizzle and tan, free from black penciling on toes. Height: 15 in. Weight: 20 lbs.

This is a well-built, game, plucky terrier, with a smart and active appearance. The skull is flat, fairly wide between the ears, and with a fairly strong muzzle. The eyes are of a dark hazel color, are small and indicate abundant pluck. Ears are V-shaped, small, set on fairly high and carried forward close to the cheek. Back should be short and well ribbed, and the hind-quarters strong and the thighs muscular. The tail is set on high and should not be carried too gaily. The coat is wiry, hard, very close and abundant. White patches should disqualify.

SEALYHAM TERRIER

Color: White with tan or brown patches, but such are not desirable. Height: 10 in. Weight: 16 lbs.

This dog was formerly known as the Border or Cowley terrier, and has within recent years become very popular on account of his workmanlike terrier qualifications. He should possess a long head with punishing jaw, and be endowed with abundant whiskers. His ears are carried like the fox terrier's, eye small and dark, well sprung ribs, body fairly long, immense bone for his size, short on the leg and hard weather-resisting coat.

[34]

WELSH SPRINGER

Color: Red or orange and white.
Weight: Not more than 42 lbs.

As a worker this dog has no superior. He owns a well balanced head, grand spring of rib, and powerful hind quarters. He may best be described as a large Cocker Spaniel. His eyes should be hazel or dark brown and should not show any haw. The ears are comparatively small and hang close to the cheeks. His coat is straight or flat and thick.

The Welsh Springer has been bred and preserved in its purity for hundreds of years. As a worker he has no superior, no day being too long and no covert too difficult for the endurance and pluck of the gay Cambrian Springer.

WELSH HOUND

Color: Grizzle-red with white patches and with white markings like the English Foxhound, Harrier and Beagle.
Height: 24 in.
Weight: 75 lbs.

A symmetrically built dog on racy lines. His head is of good length, domed in skull and rather long muzzle. The eyes are small, brown and intelligent in expression. The ears are often rounded and lay close to the head. Neck long, clean and muscular without dewlap. Back strong and broad, deep in the chest and very muscular in thighs and hind-quarters. Tail should be carried gaily, thick at the root and well furnished with hard hair. The coat is hard, wiry, crisp and water resisting.

British Colonial Breeds

GAZELLE HOUND (India)
LHASSA TERRIER (India)
TIBETAN MASTIFF (India)
RAMPUR GREYHOUND (India)
BANJARA (India)
BARB (Australia)
AUSTRALIAN TERRIER (Australia)

KANGAROO GREYHOUND (Australia)
MALTESE TERRIER (Malta)
NEWFOUNDLAND, Black (Newfoundland)
NEWFOUNDLAND, other than Black (Newfoundland)
HUSKIE (Canada)
LABRADOR (Canada)

GAZELLE

Color: Self-colored black and the different shades of fawn and dirty white.
Height: 29 in.
Weight: 70 lbs.
A big dog built on delicate and elegant lines. The head is fine, lean and bony. Skull long and slightly domed. Eyes mild, intelligent and dark brown, like the gazelle. Ears are long, hang close to the head and are abundantly coated. The neck is long, chest deep, back straight, long and strong, and tail is of fair length. The coat is smooth and very soft and the ears and tail are covered with long, wavy, silky hair.

LHASSA TERRIER

Color: Black, dark grizzle, slate, sandy, or mixture of these colors with white.
Height: About 11 in.
Weight: About 14 lbs.

The head is distinctly terrier-like, with narrow skull, which falls away in a marked degree behind the eyes. The eyes are dark brown in color. Ears set on low and carried close to the cheeks. Body not too short, and well ribbed up. The legs are short, with a tendency to crookedness. The tail is carried over the back. A low carriage is considered a sign of impure blood. The coat is of good length, straight and very dense with a strong growth on the skull, and the legs should be well coated right down to the toes.

TIBETAN MASTIFF

Color: Black and tan, red with black saddle, mahogany red, or all black. White is sometimes seen on the chest and toes.
Height: Not less than 30 in. Weight: Not less than 160 lbs.

This is a large, powerful and noble-looking animal, in aspect courageous, grim and earnest. The skull is broad and arched, with prominent occiput. His small eyes are dark brown in color, and often show the haw. The deep wrinkles around the eyes give him a sullen, savage look. Ears set on high, hang straight down, and not too long. His neck is short and powerful, the hair on it standing up like a mane. The tail is short, bushy and usually carried over the back, and his coat is soft, thick, long and straight, with a woolly undercoat.

[37]

RAMPUR GREYHOUND

Color: Mouse-gray. Height: 30 in. Weight: 75 lbs.
This is a powerfully-built greyhound, with a long, strong skull, flat between the ears, without any stop and has powerful jaws. His light yellow eyes give him a hard and cruel expression. His ears are fairly large and are Filbert-shaped. The body is somewhat coarse, of fair length. Chest very deep and back slightly arched. When in action the tail is carried horizontally and the end slightly curled upwards. His coat is like that of a freshly clipped horse, if longer is a sign of impure blood.

BANJARA

Color: Self-colored, sandy, light fawn, and the various shades of gray. Without white if possible, but a little white on chest and toes does not disqualify.
Height: 25 in.
Weight: 45 lbs.
This dog is indigenous to the North of India, is as hard as nails in constitution, somewhat rough and rugged in outlook, but a well-built, symmetrical dog, possessed of considerable speed. His expression should be very keen and wicked, especially when roused. Head is long and flat, well filled up before the eyes, with a

strong punishing jaw. The ears lay flat on the cheeks and are filbert shaped. His small eye is close set, and the color varies to the shade of the dog's coat. The body is moderately long and falls away a good deal to the set-on of the tail, which also is set on low and carried with an upward sweep. His coat is very thick and dense and close lying, soft to the touch but not silky.

[38]

BARB
(The Australian Sheep Dog, often called the Kelpie)

Color: All black.
Height: 24 in.
Weight: 54 lbs.

A well-built, medium-sized dog with a head like the Pomeranian or Schipperke. His almond-shaped, dark eyes convey an intelligent expression. The ears are pricked, neck long and well arched, back straight, chest deep but not too wide, and well developed loins. The tail is of medium length and carried rather high, and his coat is of fair length, straight and harsh.

This dog is extensively used by Australian and New Zealand shepherds in the work-a-day life on their sheep ranches. His intelligence and adaptability as a working sheep dog is said to be even more pronounced than the best English, Welsh or Scotch exponents. Furthermore, he has been bred in some quarters so that he cannot bark.

AUSTRALIAN TERRIER

Color: Blue or gray body, tan on legs or face, with a top-knot of blue or silver. Clear sandy or deep red.
Height: 10 in.
Weight: 15 lbs.

This is a rather low set dog, compact and active. The head is long, full between the eyes with a top-knot of soft hair. Eyes small, keen and of dark color. Ears small, set high on skull, free from long hairs, and may be either cropped or uncropped. The tail is docked. The coat should be straight and of wiry texture.

[39]

KANGAROO GREYHOUND

Color: All colors. Black not desirable.
Height: 29 in.
Weight: 66 lbs.

In general appearance he resembles the English Greyhound, but is heavier built. The skull is broader between the ears and more domed and the ears are not set so high as those of the English dog. His eyes are brown and intelligent. Neck slender, muscular and slightly arched. Back long and strong, with short, arched and muscular loins, and his hindquarters are well developed and very muscular. The tail is long and fine and carried downwards and his coat is smooth and fine, though sometimes coarser on the body.

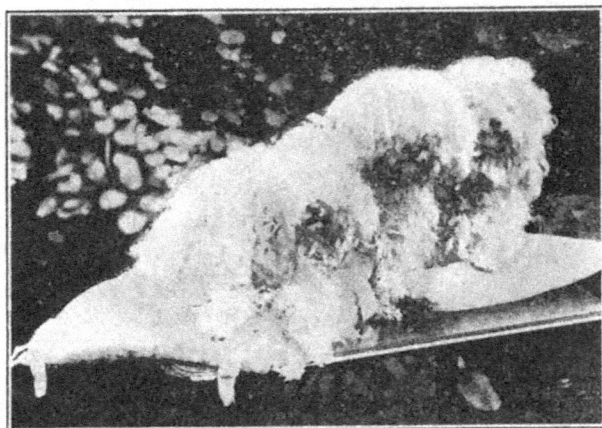

MALTESE

Color: Pure white, without
Height: From 8 to 12 in.
Weight: Under 12 lbs.;

This is a bright, spritely, act.. ..., tai.ing character. His head is much like that of a drop-eared Skye Terrier in miniature, but rather shorter and thicker in muzzle. The ears are moderately long and are covered with long, silky hair, and his eyes are very dark and piercing. He is short and cobby in back, and legginess should be avoided. The tail is short, well feathered, particularly towards the end, and carried gracefully over the back.

[40]

NEWFOUNDLAND (Black)

Color: A. Jet black with a slight tinge of brown or a splash of white on chest and toes is not objectionable. B. Black and white, or white and black. Beauty in markings is of great consideration. C. Self-colored bronze.

Height: 27 in. or more.

Weight: 100 lbs. or more.

This dog should impress the eye with strength and great activity. He is a free mover for his size and should be sound on his legs. The head is broad, massive, flat, with the occiput well developed. There is no decided stop and the muzzle should be short and rather square in shape. The eyes are small, dark brown, showing no haw, and set widely apart. Small ears set well back and covered with short hair without fringe. He should be massive in bone, well ribbed up in body, with broad back and strong loins and hind quarters. Dew claws are objectionable. The tail is of moderate length and should be well covered with long hair, carried downwards when in repose. Tails with a kink in them or curled over the back are very objectionable.

NEWFOUNDLAND (Black and white)

The Huskie Sledge Dogs of Northern Canada

The Huskie is a strong, powerfully built dog, varying in size and color, but uniform as to his great bone, stamina and dense coat. He is extensively used for all manner of draught work in which service he has made himself indispensable to mankind in the northern latitudes. See special chapter on Alaskan dogs.

THE LABRADOR RETRIEVER

Color: Black.
Height: 26 in.
Weight: 80 lbs.

The Labrador is of medium size, strong and well built, head strong and rather long with wide. rather flat skull with a slight ridge running down it. The eyes should be oval in shape, dark brown in color and of gentle and intelligent expression. Being a hard working dog the body should be rather long and well ribbed up, and deep in the brisket. He should carry his thick and bushy tail rather high but not on the back, his coat should be very profuse, and of moderate length, lying close to the body and very oily.

French Breeds

Pyrenean Sheepdog
French Sheepdog
Barbet
Smooth-Coated Basset
Rough-Coated Basset
Rough-Coated Basset of Brittany
Basset of Ardennes
Rough-Coated Basset of Vendée
Blue Basset of Gascogne
French Pointer
Dupuy Pointer
Pointer of Ariège
Pointer of Saint-Germain
Pointer Bourbonnais
Blue Pointer of Auvergne
French Setter
Setter of Picardie
Setter of Pont-Audemer
Griffon Boulet

Griffon Guerlain
Griffon Nivernais
Griffon Fauve de Bretagne
Griffon Vendéen
French Bulldog
Non-Corded Poodle
Corded Poodle
Toy Poodle.
Bordeaux
Hound of Vendée
Poitevin Hound
Poitou Hound
Normand Dog
Saintonge
Gascogne
Franche-Comté
Artois
Virelade
Gris de Saint-Louis

PYRENEAN SHEEPDOG

Color. All white, sometimes with small orange patches on the ears.
Height: 30 in. Weight: 155 lbs.

This is a large, well-built dog, with a rather weak head in comparison to his body. The skull is slightly rounded, and the muzzle should not be too square. The small eyes should be brown and set obliquely in the head. Ears of medium size, hanging close to the head. The tail is long, well feathered and carried low, and his coat is long, straight, dense, and fitting close to the body.

FRENCH SHEEPDOG

Color: Dirty black, slate, grizzle and reddish.
Height: 25 in.
Weight: 65 lbs.

This is a well-built dog of medium size, with a busy and intelligent appearance, and is well covered with a shaggy coat. The head is strong and covered with long hair, forming eyebrows, beard and whiskers, yet the eye is not hidden by the hair. The eyes are brown and very expressive, ears short, erect and never pendulous and often cut. Body is well-built for endurance. The tail is never docked, of medium length and carried low, and his coat is long and woolly.

BARBET

Color: Grizzle black, creamy brown, dirty white, white and chestnut, and white and black.
Height: 22 in.
Weight: 56 lbs.

The Barbet is a strongly made dog, very compactly built. Is round and broad in skull with forehead well developed. Muzzle broad and short, well furnished with long moustaches. The eyes are round, lively and intelligent and dark brown in color, and are entirely hidden by the long and thick hair on the eyebrows. The ears are set on low, are long and flat and well covered with long, curly hair, which often forms cords or ringlets. The body is strongly built, ribs and loins well rounded and muscular. The forelegs are straight with plenty of bone and covered with long hair. The tail is set on low, carried slightly upwards. The Barbet's coat is long, woolly and curly, forming cords or ringlets.

SMOOTH-COATED FRENCH BASSET HOUND

Color: Black with white and tan, the head, shoulders and quarters a rich tan, and black patches on the back. They are sometimes hare-pied.

Height: 13 in.

Weight: 50 lbs.

The head is most perfect when it closely resembles that of a bloodhound. It is long and narrow with heavy flues, prominent occiput, and forehead wrinkled to the eyes. The general appearance of the head should indicate high breeding and a reproachful dignity. The eyes show a kind expression and no haw is visible. Ears very long, so long that in hunting they will often actually tread on them, set on low, and hang loose in folds like drapery. Their texture is thin and velvety. Forelegs only about four inches long. Stern is carried hound fashion, coat short, fine, smooth and glossy. Skin is loose and elastic.

ROUGH-COATED FRENCH BASSET HOUND

Color: Any recognized hound color.

Height: 13 in.

Weight: 50 lbs.

A very powerful hound for its size, on short and strong legs. The head is large, skull long and narrow and peak well developed. A snipy or weak jaw is objectionable. The eyes are dark with a kindly and intelligent expression. Ears set on low, of good length and fine in texture. Chest large and very deep. Body massive, of good length, any weakness or lightness of loin being a bad fault. Forelegs are short and very powerful. Stern of moderate length and carried gaily. The coat is profuse, thick and harsh to the touch, with a dense undercoat, and may be wavy.

[45]

ROUGH-COATED BASSET OF BRITTANY

Color: Tawny-red with white markings.
Height: 12 in.
Weight: 56 lbs.
This is a coarse looking dog with long body and short, heavy neck. The head is long with high domed skull. Stop slightly developed and long muzzle. The eyes are dark in color, ears long, rounded at the tips and slightly folded. Stern of medium length and carried upwards. The coat is wiry and broken, of fair length, softer on the skull and ears.

BASSET OF THE ARDENNES

Color: Black and tan, hare color or tawny red.
Height: 15 in.
Weight: 55 lbs.
This is a typical hound, a bloodhound in miniature. The head is large but not broad, skull high and narrow, occipital bone well developed, with pendulous lips. Eyes brown, with eye lids loose and pendulous. The ears are long, fine and hanging forward close to the jaws. Body is heavy and massive and the back long, broad and deep. The stern is carried hound-like. The coat is short, hard on the body, but softer on the ears and skull.

[46]

ROUGH-COATED BASSET OF VENDÉE

Color: White with red patches or tri-color.
Height: 15 in.
Weight: 56 lbs.
This is a dog of strong and muscular shape, with a long, lean, slightly rounded head. The eyes are dark brown with an intelligent outlook and somewhat hidden by the strong eyebrows. The ears are soft, flat and covered with white hair. Body long and low, and deep in chest. The stern is short, set on high and carried very gaily. The coat is hard but of rather fine texture.

BLUE BASSET OF GASCOGNE

Color: Tri-color, so-called trout color, blue-mottled, white with black and light tan spots above the eyes.
Height: 14 in.
Weight: 56 lbs.
This is a strong and massive dog, with a long, well developed head, skull high and narrow, prominent occiput and lips not too pendulous. The eyes are dark brown, ears very long and folded. He is long in body, with broad and deep chest. The stern is fine, set on low, and carried upwards, and his coat is short and dense.

[47]

FRENCH POINTER
The stern is generally docked; in all other respects similar to the English Pointer.

DUPUY POINTER
Color: Pure white with small or large dull brown markings.
Height: 27 in. Weight: 50 lbs.
The Dupuy Pointer is a big upstanding dog with considerable elegance in his movements. The head is narrow and long. Occipital bone prominent, muzzle long, lean and slightly arched. Eyes golden brown in color with a rather melancholy expression. Nose well developed and broad and brown in color. Lips fine, thin and very tight. Ears set on rather high, very fine in texture, not too long, and folded backwards. The neck is long and gracefully arched. Chest deep and narrow. Hindquarters strong and muscular. Stern long, set low and carried like a greyhound's tail.

POINTER OF ARIEGE

Color: White with light brown or lemon spots.
Height: 26 in.
Weight: 70 lbs.
This dog is elegant in build and well developed. The skull should be rather narrow with the occipital bone well defined. Muzzle long with a slight stop. Lips thin and pendulous. Ears very thin, long and set on low. Neck long, graceful, strong and free from dewlaps. Chest broad and deep, long in the back and loins. Hindquarters muscular and well developed. The tail is long, set on rather low, and generally docked.

POINTER OF SAINT-GERMAIN

Color: White with large lemon markings, not spots.
Height: 27 in.
Weight: 60 lbs.
In general appearance he is a clever looking, graceful dog, symmetrical in shape and standing rather high on the leg. The occipital bone should be well developed. Skull rather broad. Stop well defined, and the muzzle long and straight. Eyes golden or yellow in color. Ears set on high, shorter than the ears of the French Pointer, but longer than the ears of the English Pointer. The neck is strong and well arched; chest deep and broad. Hindquarters muscular and fully developed. Tail thick at the root, carried straight or with a little curve but no curl at the tip.

[49]

POINTER BOUR- BONNAIS

Color: White with light chestnut spots, and no large markings.
Height: 24 in.
Weight: 70 lbs.
This dog is rather lighter in bone than the English and French varieties, is shorter and more compact in build, and more of the appearance of a cob. The head should be long, straight and rather broad; eyes large, dark amber in color, and with an intelligent expression. Ears fine and not too long, set on rather low and hanging in folds. Neck strong, short and muscular. Chest deep and broad. Hindquarters short, round and muscular. Stern set on rather low, and not more than 3 inches in length.

BLUE POINTER OF AUVERGNE

Color: White with black markings and tickings, giving a blue effect. Head always black with a white blaze up the face.
Height: 25 in.
Weight: 53 lbs.
In general appearance this dog is of perfect proportions suitable for hard work. The occipital bone should be well defined. Skull broad with a pronounced dip below the eyes. Muzzle straight and cheek bones well developed. The eyes should be dark brown in color. Lips very pendulous. Ears long and fine in texture, hanging in folds and should be set on level with the eyes and not carried too closely to the head. Neck strong, slightly arched and throaty. Hindquarters and legs similar to other varieties of the Pointer. Stern strong at the root and generally docked and set on low.

FRENCH SETTER

Color: White with chestnut patches.
Height: 25 in.
Weight: 56 lbs.
The French Setter is a strong, shapely dog of an imposing appearance. The head is strong and well developed. Skull round, broad and long with the occipital bone well defined and the stop nicely chiselled. The eyes should be rather small, dark amber in color, and of open expression. His chest should be very deep and broad with long and rather flat ribs. The stern set on high, rather long and be carried in two curves; the first convex and the second concave, with a nice fringe of long, wavy, silky hair. His coat should be thick and not bright, smooth on the head and flat on the body with a fair amount on the belly, chest and throat and the ears and legs well feathered.

SETTER OF PICARDIE

This is a variety of the French Setter and is sometimes called the black Setter of the North. The points are the same, except that in color he should be brown and grizzle, black or black and tan.

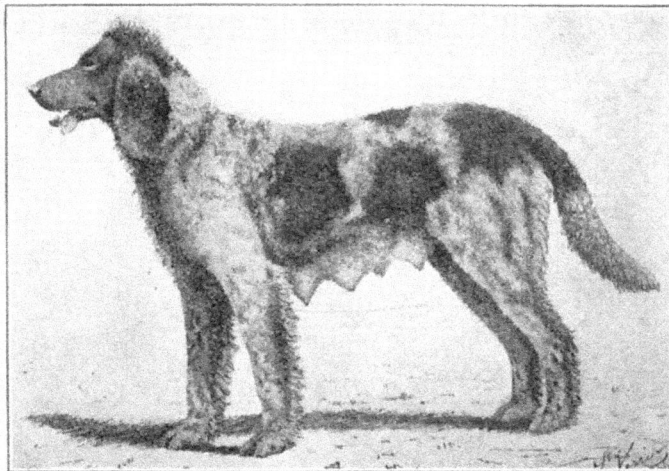

SETTER OF PONT-AUDEMER

Color: Brown and grizzle, brown and white, or self-colored brown. A black or black and white coat is objectionable.
Height: 22 in.
Weight: 56 lbs.
This dog should be of a short, thick-set build with a cobby appearance. The skull should be round with prominent occipital bone, forehead rising well toward the top knot or crest. Eyes dark amber with a good and frank expression. Nose brown and nostrils well open. The ears should be set on rather low, hanging close to the neck and should be very long and well furnished with long, crisp hair. The chest is deep and broad, back and loins strong and muscular; back slightly convex, strong and short. The stern should be strong in bone at the root, carried rather straight and is generally docked. The coat should be crisp on the ears and top knot, which should stand upright, and rather thick and curly on the body. The hair on mask should be smooth.

GRIFFON BOULET

Color: Chestnut, dead leaf color with or without white, never with black or yellow. Height: 23 in. Weight: 56 lbs.

A rather coarse-looking dog, but with a sharp appearance and his expression is mild and intelligent. Has broad and round skull, long, broad and square muzzle, with heavy moustaches. The "stop" well defined but accentuated by strong eyebrows, give him a rather savage aspect. The eyes, however, are intelligent and affable, of yellow color. The nose is light color or brown with nostrils well open. The chest is broad and deep and the ribs well arched. The forelegs are strong and muscular, covered with abundance of long hair. The straight tail is of medium length, well covered with hair but no feathering. His coat is of a nondescript character, fairly long, and silky without brilliancy and smooth or wavy, but is never curly.

GRIFFON GUERLAIN

Color: White with orange or yellow patches.
Height: 23 in.
Weight: 56 lbs.

This is a medium-sized dog, short in the body and compactly built. He has a big head for his size and the eyes are rather large and light brown in color. The nose is always brown with nostrils well open. Chest broad and back strong and well developed. The legs are straight and muscular, rather on the long side and well covered with short, wiry hair. Stern is carried straight, covered with wiry hair but without feathering, and a third of its length is generally docked. The coat is hard and wiry, rather short and not curly.

GRIFFON NIVERNAIS

Color. Tri-color, black and tan and brown, with or without dirty white patches.
Height: 23 in.
Weight: 60 lbs.

A strongly built dog, rather long in body and not particularly attractive in appearance. The head is fairly long and rather square with slightly domed skull. Muzzle also of medium length and of square formation. The eyes are bright, intelligent and brown in color. Ears set high and well back on the head, of good size and hanging without folds close to the head. Back long, straight and muscular, as also are the loins. The legs are straight with plenty of bone and covered with hard hair. Stern of medium length, also well covered with hair. The coat is semi-long, close and of a hard texture.

GRIFFON FAUVE DE BRETAGNE

Color: Fallow, inclined to red, sometimes discolored red.
Height: 23 in.
Weight: 65 lbs.

A heavily-built dog, very robust. The head is large and strong with flat skull, prominent occiput and muzzle of good length, square and strong. The ears should not be too long and are covered with soft hair. The neck is short and muscular and the chest deep. He is endowed with plenty of bone in the leg and has splendid feet. The stern is of medium length, well covered with hair but not any feathering. The coat is semi-long, hard and wiry.

[53]

GRIFFON VENDEEN

Color: White and orange, white and wheaten, white and mouse-gray, and with red or brown patches.
Height: 25 in.
Weight: 65 lbs.
An upstanding dog of firm structure, covered with a hard and close coat. The head is rather big and typical, pronounced in occiput and muzzle of good length. The eyes are rather small, brown in color and full of life. Ears long, nicely folded and hang gracefully. He is muscular in body, deep and broad in chest with a rather long muscular back. The stern is of medium length, carried gaily and well covered with hard hair. The coat is thick, hard and wiry.

A similar dog to the Vendeen but more nervous in temperament and not so heavily coated as the Griffon de Cosse, and those marked with the red or brown patches are called Griffons du Grip or Griffons d'Anjou.

FRENCH BULLDOG

Color: Almost any color, but black and black and tan will disqualify.
Weight: Three classes are provided, under 20 lbs., 20 to 24 lbs., and 24 to 28 lbs.
The French Bulldog ought to have the appearance of an active, intelligent and very muscular dog of cobby build and heavy in the bone for his size. The head should be large and square with the forehead nearly flat, the muscles of the cheek well developed but not prominent. "Stop" as deep as possible. The forehead should be wrinkled, and the skin of the head not tight. Eyes moderate in size and dark in color. "Bat" ears of medium size, large at the base and rounded at the tips and placed high on the head. The body should be short and rotund with a distinct roach and light but sound quarters. His shoulders should be strong and he should stand on short but fairly stout limbs for his size. The fundamental difference between the French Bulldog and the English miniature is seen in the foreface which in the French should show some slight protusion of the underjaw, and some turnup, but no layback.

CORDED POODLE

Color: All black, all white, all red, or all blue.
Height: 22 in.
Weight: 50 lbs.

The most popular varieties of the Poodle are the corded and non-corded. In general appearance he presents an active and elegant outline. He is a well-built dog and carries himself proudly. The head is long, straight and fine. The muzzle should be strong and the lips black and fit tightly. Eyes almond shape, very dark brown, and full of fire and intelligence. The ears are long and wide, set on high and hang close to the head. The back is strong and muscular. The tail is set on high and should never be curled or carried over the back. In the corded variety the white Poodle should have dark eyes, black or dark liver nose, lips and toe nails. The red Poodle should have dark amber eyes, with dark liver nose, lips and toe nails. The blue Poodle should be of even color, without patches of black or white, and have dark eyes, lips and toe nails. All the other points of the white, red and blue Poodle should be the same as the perfect black Poodle. The coat should be very profuse, of good, hard texture, hanging in tight, even cords. In the non-corded variety the coat should be very profuse, of hard texture of even length, and may be either curly or fluffy.

NON-CORDED POODLE

[55]

TOY POODLE

Similar in all respects to the non-corded variety, but the coat is softer and silkier, and he should not stand more than 12 inches high or weigh more than 10 pounds.

BORDEAUX

Color: Reddish fawn, with red mask, red with red mask, fawn and no mask fawn or red with black mask. Brindles, blacks and pied disqualify.

Height: 29 in.

Weight: 120 lbs.

This is a smooth-coated dog, very powerful in build, somewhat low in stature massive, broad and muscular. He possesses an enormous head, greater in proportion to his body than that of any other breed, and should be very long and broad, high and square, and the whole of the face and muzzle should be covered with ropes of loose skin, lying in wrinkles. The eyes are small, wide apart, deep set, light in color, and very penetrating in expression. The "rose" ears when uncropped should be small and fine in texture. The neck is very thick and powerful, with skin very loose, forming a dewlap on each side of the throat. Back is short and straight, of great breadth at the shoulder, and the hindquarters should be pear-shaped, as in the bulldog, and it should not be forgotten that this dog is the gladiator of his race.

HOUND OF VENDÈE

Color: White or with dark red and yellow patches. Height: 28 in. Weight: 58 lbs. A strong dog, well built and elegant. His head is clean and slightly arched and skull rounded. The eyes are dark yellow or dark brown in color. Nose brown with well open nostrils. The ears are flexible, thin, long, pendulous, set on low and nicely folded. The neck is long, clean, well muscled and splendidly arched. The loins are well arched, powerful and deep.. Legs clean, straight and well boned and stern of medium length, tapering and carried rather high. The coat is short and fine.

POITEVIN HOUND

Color: White, blue and orange, with pale tan markings on body and legs.

Height: 25 in.

Weight: 58 lbs.

This is a muscular sort of dog with rather square fine head, slightly domed in skull, occipital bone not particularly well developed. Eyes are brown and intelligent. Nose black with open nostrils. Ears well set on, rather short and well folded. Neck of good length. Back slightly arched and chest not too deep. The legs are straight, strong and well boned. Stern of medium length, carried gaily and with a short, rather thick coat.

[57]

POITOU HOUND

Color: White, black and tan, and tri-color.

Height: 26 in.
Weight: 58 lbs.

A muscular dog with limbs rather flat but large. The head is lean, fine and carried proudly on a well arched neck. The skull is slightly domed and the occipital bone just visible, and the muzzle should be long. The brown eyes give him a bright and intelligent expression. The ears are moderately short, very thin, velvety and hang gracefully in folds. His deep chest, slightly arched back, well muscled loins and straight, well-boned limbs, fit him for arduous work. The stern is of medium length and tapers towards the point. The coat is coarse and should not be too short, especially on hindquarters and stern.

NORMAND DOG

Color: White with large brown, black or grizzled patches, tri-color with grizzle saddle. Height: 29 in. Weight: 78 lbs.

A heavy, strong, rather coarse-looking dog and is the heaviest of all the French Hounds. He has a long, broad skull with coarse muzzle and the skin on the head is very loose and wrinkled. The eyes are full and gay and the haw is visible. Ears set on low, long, thin, velvety and folding inwards. The body is rather long and heavy. Neck short, strong and thick with heavy dewlap. Back broad, strong and well muscled. Legs strong, muscular and with rather coarse bone. The feet are clean and pointed. The stern is thick at the root, tapering towards the point and carried gaily, curved upwards. The coat is short and coarse in appearance.

[58]

SAINTONGE

Color: White with black patches and blue belton. The ears and palate always black and he has light tan spots above the eyes. Height: 28 in. Weight: 62 lbs.

In general appearance this dog is elegant and not too heavily built. The head is lean, light and of a fair length, with skull slightly arched and with occipital bone well developed. The eyes are bright and intelligent, showing the haw and brown in color. Ears long, fine, set on low, black in color, edged with a light tan. Chest deep and rather narrow; legs straight, lean and rather long. Stern is of medium length and tapering. Coat short and fine.

GASCOGNE

Color: Blue or white with many black spots, blue mottled, and pale tan markings, rather black and the legs tinted with red. Height: 23 in. Weight: 55 lbs.

This is a strong and massive dog, with a large and sometimes a rather long head, with the occipital bone well developed, resembling in this respect a bloodhound. The eyes are brown, bright and clear, and somewhat hidden, showing the haw. The lips are pendulous. Ears very long, rather fine and well folded. Chest very deep, back broad and strong. The stern is fine but not too long and carried well up. Coat short and hard on the body, soft and silky on the skull and ears.

FRANCHE-COMTÈ

Color: White with yellow, orange or red patches.
Height: 23 in.
Weight: 54 lbs.

A dog of medium size and symmetrically built. The head is fine and of fair length with domed skull and the occipital bone slightly developed. Eyes of medium size, bright and brown in color. Ears are set on low, of medium length, thin and soft. He is rather short in the neck, chest deep, ribs not too rounded, legs well boned and muscular. His stern is set on high, rather short, and tapers to a fine point. The coat is smooth, fine and glossy.

ARTOIS

Color: White with yellow or red patches, tri-color with black saddle.
Height: 23 in.
Weight: 50 lbs.

A strong and well-built dog of medium size. Rather long skull, with the stop not too deep. The eyes are full, dark yellow or light brown in color. The ears are broad, very long and set on low. Body not too long, neck rather short, back strong and straight. His legs are not too long and are straight and strong. The stern is strong and carried upwards. The coat is short and not too silky.

VIRELADE

Color: White with large black patches and light tan spots.
Height: About 29 in.
Weight: About 62 lbs.
A dog of great size, yet strong and light and rather long in the body. The head is fine rather than heavy; occipital bone well developed, and has pendulous lips. The eyes are brown in color and the ears long and fine. He is strong, straight and well boned in the legs. The stern is long and carried hound-like, and he is short in coat.

GRIS DE SAINT-LOUIS

Color: Grizzle on the back, red brindled with the legs of a hare color, or the back rather black and the legs tinted with red. Height: 23 in. Weight: 55 lbs.
This is a dog of good size, rather high on the legs, strong and symmetrically built. The long, well-developed head has a broad skull, slightly rounded and stop well defined. The muzzle is of medium length, square and strong. His bright and intelligent eyes are dark brown in color. The ears are set well back on the head, are long, thin, and nicely folded. Neck not too long and very muscular. He is strong and broad in back with a deep and capacious chest. Legs straight, long and well boned. The stern is thick and well covered with hair and carried very curved. The coat is hard and wiry.

German Breeds

GREAT DANE	SMOOTH-COATED GERMAN POINTER
DACHSHUND	ROUGH-COATED GERMAN POINTER
POMERANIAN	POINTER OF WURTEMBERG
POMERANIAN (Miniature)	POINTER OF WEIMAR
DOBERMANN PINSCHER	GERMAN SETTER
AFFENPINSCHER	WACHTELHUND
GERMAN SHEEP DOG	GRIFFON-KORTHALS
GERMAN HOUND	BOXER
WIRE-COATED GERMAN TERRIER	HANOVRIAN LIMER
SMOOTH-COATED GERMAN TERRIER	BAVARIAN LIMER

GREAT DANE

Color: Brindle, fawn, blue, black and harlequin. The harlequin should have jet-black patches and spots on a pure white ground.

Height: 30 in. or more. Weight: 120 lbs. and over.

This dog is remarkable in size and very muscular. Strongly yet elegantly built, which latter feature is an absolute essential, as also is alertness of expresion and brisk-ness of movement, and generally he should carry a look of dash and daring. The head is of great length, muzzle broad, and jaw powerful. The skull should be flat rather than domed, and have a slight indentation running up the center. The ears in Germany are cropped, set high, and carried erect, with the tips falling forward. The neck should be long and well arched, and quite free from loose skin. The body is very deep, back strong and hind quarters extremely muscular. His coat is short, dense and sleek.

The abolition of cropping by the English Kennel Club resulted in English breeders concentrating their attention to the production of a small ear, which would hang neatly in lieu of his original large ear, which was desirable when cropping was per-mitted. In doing this, character was at first lost, to some extent, in head, color and soundness of limb, but these temporary disabilities have now been largely overcome.

[62]

DACHSHUND

Color: Black, gray, red or yellow in good harmony, much white is objectionable. Height: English standard, 7 to 9 in.; German standard, 7 to 8½ in. Weight: English standard, 18 to 21 lbs.; German standard, three classes: A, 15½ to 16½ lbs.; B, 15 to 22 lbs.; C, Over 22 lbs.

It will be observed from the above that there is a difference of opinion between the German and English ideas as to the most desirable size of the Dachshund. This dog is of a long, low and graceful conformation. His figure though elongated should present a stiff and muscular appearance, notwithstanding his short and crooked front. He should not appear lean or weasel-like. His pert, saucy pose of the head are desirable characteristics. The skull is long and narrow, eyes small and in shade should follow the color of the dog, ears long, broad and soft, chest narrow and deep with breast bone prominent, stern long and strong, flat at the root and carried low. His skin should be thick, subtle, loose and in great quantity. There are three varieties as regards coat. A—The smooth, short and strong coat. B—The rough, dense, not silky or long coat. C—The long-coated variety, which should be straight, though it is sometimes wavy, fine and glossy. It should be abundant on the neck, chest, ears, forelegs and tail.

It is worthy of notice that though the Dachshund is of German origin, the English Dachshund Club, founded in 1881, preceded the German Teckel Klub by ten years, and Dachshunds were exhibited in England five or six years before they made their appearance on the show bench in Germany. The "points" of the two clubs also differed considerably, more particularly in regard to the head and size. The English breeders seemed rather to regard him as a hound, but now-a-days there is little or no difference between the best specimens of the two countries.

POMERANIAN
(Spitz)

Color: White, black, blue, brown, chocolate, sable in all shades, red, orange and fawn in all shades, and parti-colors. The whites must be free from lemon or any color, and the other colors free from white. In the parti-colors the colors should be evenly distributed in body patches. Self colored dogs with white feet or legs are objectionable.

Weight: About 24 lbs.

This is a compact, short-bodied dog, with head and face fox-like. Small erect ears, and exhibits great intelligence in expression, docility in disposition and activity in buoyancy and deportment. The skull should be somewhat flat, eyes oblique, not set too wide apart, bright and dark in color. The neck is short and lion-like, is covered with a profuse mane and frill of long straight hair. The tail is a characteristic of the breed and should be turned over the back, profusely covered with long spreading hair. He should have a long, perfectly straight and glistening coat, sound and even in color and soft fluffy undercoat, the whole effect being of a stand-off, weather resisting variety.

POMERANIAN
(Miniature)

This breed has now been per-fected as a toy variety to the almost entire exclusion from the show ring of the original spitz. Formerly he was pro-duced in Pomeria, in all sizes from 20 to 40 lbs. weight. Then the fashionable weight became 18 to 24 lbs., but latterly breed-ers have perfected the variety and he is classified at shows as above 8 lbs. and less than 8 lbs., until nowadays the smaller they are the more they are appreciated. There are many poms around three or four pounds weight, and some full grown specimens have been exhibited as small as 1½ lbs.

[64]

DOBERMANN PINSCHER

Color: Black and tan, small white patches on chest is permissible.
Height: 24 in.
Weight: 45 lbs.

This is a well built muscular dog, with an appearance denoting quickness, strength and endurance, and he has a lively and game temperament. The skull is broad, flat and slightly rounded, muzzle long and moderately tapered. Ears well cropped and not too pointed. Eyes dark brown, of medium size, with a friendly and intelligent outlook. The back is straight and of fair length, with well developed and muscular hind quarters. The tail is docked to the length of about 6 inches, and bob-tails are much appreciated. He has a short, hard, and close-lying coat.

AFFENPINSCHER
(Monkey Terrier)

Color: Gray-black, blue-gray, dirty yellow, red and their different shades. The light-colored dogs have often a black muzzle.
Height: Not more than 20 in.
Weight: Under 8½ lbs.

This is a small ladies' dog, well built, of compact form and very intelligent. The head is thick and round, covered with long, hard and ⸺ hair, ⸺ short and strong and he should be under-shot, yet without showing ⸺ eeth, and well furnished with mustache and beard. The eyes are large, round, ⸺ inent and very intelligent and dark in color. The eyebrows should be straight ⸺ d but not hanging, with a general outlook that of the monkey. The ears are ⸺ s cut, carried erect and pointed, set on wide apart and well covered with short

He has a very compact body, is sort in neck and broad in chest. The tail is ⸺ ed to about two-thirds of its length, and is carried upwards. His coat is profuse, ⸺ hard and unequal, and should be of a dry nature, with a woolly undercoat some- ⸺ curled.

[65]

GERMAN SHEPHERD DOG

Color: Black, grizzle, reddish brown, either self colored or with tan, white white with large dark patches or brindle, with or without tan markings. White the chest and legs is permissible, but not desirable. Height: 22 in. Weight: 55 l

This is a medium sized dog, rather long in the body but well built, and is v game and intelligent. The head is lean, skull broad between the ears and long l muzzle. The ears are of medium size, carried erect, and pointed forward. The e are almond shaped, dark in color, full of "fire" and intelligence, but often sour. body is rather narrow, with deep chest, straight back and strong loins. The tai well coated, carried low when the dog is quiet and gaily but not over the back w excited. There are three varieties as to coat: A. Smooth coated. Short dense hard, round the neck the coat is longer and harder. B. Long haired, wavy and ha the hair on the head partially covering the eyes, and with well marked beard moustaches and tail well feathered. C. Wire haired. Straight, hard and wiry, on the head and legs being especially short and hard with beard and eyebrows developed.

GERMAN HOUND

Color: White muzzle, collar, neck, chest and tip of tail; the head, body and tail are orange, tawny, yellow, black, grizzle or brindle, but never brown.

Height: 21 in.
Weight: 40 lbs.

This is a lightly made, elegant dog, with head lean, long and narrow. occipital bone not prominent, and "stop" slightly developed. The eyes are bright with a friendly expression. Ears long, broad, flat and round at the tips. Fairly light in body, which is well developed in comparison to the head. Stern long, rather thick, tapering point and well covered with long hair, and carried downwards with a slight upwards. The coat is long for a smooth coated dog and is very dense and hard.

[66]

WIRE-COATED GERMAN TERRIER
(Schnanzer or Rattler)

Color: Pepper and salt, iron-gray, silver-gray, dull black with yellow or tan markings on head and legs, rust-yellow and gray-yellow. A bright red is objectionable.

Height: 18 in.

Weight: 28 lbs.

This is a strongly built cobby dog, of a rather nervous temperament, yet he is gay, watchful, very intelligent and courageous, without being quarrelsome. He is a first rate rat dog. The head is strong, fairly long, with a flat skull rather narrow between the ears, and the occiput is well developed. The ears are set on high and are cropped with rounded tips. The oval eyes convey an intelligent and vivacious expression, with eyebrows well developed and covered with rough upstanding hair. His back is strong and straight and rather flat sided in rib. The tail is set on high, is docked very short and if a bob-tail is much appreciated. The coat is as hard, rough and wiry as possible, of the stand-off variety and though it is shorter on the head, it is not softer. On the muzzle we find a characteristic short beard and whiskers.

This breed has worked himself into popular favor in Germany by his indefatigable industry as a worker and as a good friend of the horse, hence he is much appreciated in the stable. Certainly he is very intelligent, a very apt pupil, as quick as lightning in his movements and unfailing in his fidelity, courage, endurance and muscular strength. He is a rare good dog for bad weather purposes.

SMOOTH-COATED GERMAN TERRIER

This dog is the same in every particular to the wire-coated German terrier, excepting that his color is black and tan, black with yellow shade and wolf gray, and the coat is smooth, of fine texture and lays close to the body.

[67]

SMOOTH-COATED GERMAN POINTER

Color: Pure brown, brown and white, or white with brown patches.
Height: 26 in. Weight: 70 lbs.
This dog is of medium size and is built on good uniform lines. It should not be too heavy in the head. The lips should be pendulous. Eyes oval in shape and brown in color, varying somewhat according to the shade of his coat, and have a rather grave expression. Ears moderately long but not too broad, and should lay without folds close to the head. Back straight, broad, short and muscular. The stern is of medium length, and should be carried a little above the line of the back, strong in bone at the root, but not coming to a fine point. The tail is always docked.

ROUGH-COATED GERMAN POINTER

Color: Brown and white, apparently grizzled-brown mixed with large brown markings. Height: 26 in. Weight: 70 lbs.
In general appearance this dog follows the characteristics of the smooth-coated German Pointer except in the matter of coat, which should be about 2 inches long all over the body of a rough, hard and dull texture. In the winter time a considerable undercoat is developed. The cheeks are well covered with whiskers, and the eyebrows are bushy. On the skull the hair is flat, short, hard and dull.

[68]

POINTER OF WURTEMBERG

Color: Tri-color, so-called trout color, with brown-brindle and patches of tan markings. Head and ears darker in color than the rest of the body. Height 27 in. Weight 75 lbs.

A strong, shapely dog, not coarse looking and standing rather high on the leg. The skull is long and narrow, occipital and cheek bones well developed. The eyes are light brown in color, of intelligent and grave expression and showing a prominent haw. Ears set on not too high, and hang gracefully close to the cheeks. The neck should be strong, very muscular and throaty. The chest is deep, back straight, broad and powerful, and loins broad and deep. The tail is strong and set on not too high.

POINTER OF WEIMAR

Color: Varies from silver grizzle to mouse grizzle, often clearer on the head and on the ears. White patches on the chest and on the feet are objectionable, and tan markings are decided faults.

Height: 26 in.

Weight: 70 lbs.

In general appearance the dog of Weimar is of medium size but with muscles not so well developed as the German Pointer. The head is rather light, and narrow in skull, and the occipital bone well developed. The jaws are long, lips pendulous without exaggeration, and the muzzle broad. Eyes of medium size, yellow brown in color. Nose flesh-colored, joining on to the muzzle in a clear violet tint. The ears are light and somewhat pointed. Tail rather thin and short.

[69]

GERMAN SETTER

Color: Self colored dark brown, often with a little white on chest; white with large or small brown patches or mixed; never black or red.
Height: 26 in.
Weight: 70 lbs.

In general appearance the German Setter is a strong, shapely dog, not too heavy in build. The head is rather long, skull slightly rounded, lips pendulous. Eyes are of medium size, oval in shape, dark brown in color, varying in shade with that of the coat. The body should be straight, broad and muscular, with neck slightly arched but not throaty; chest deep but not too broad. The stern should be of medium length, strong at the root and tapering near the point, carried straight to the middle with the end curled upward and well feathered.

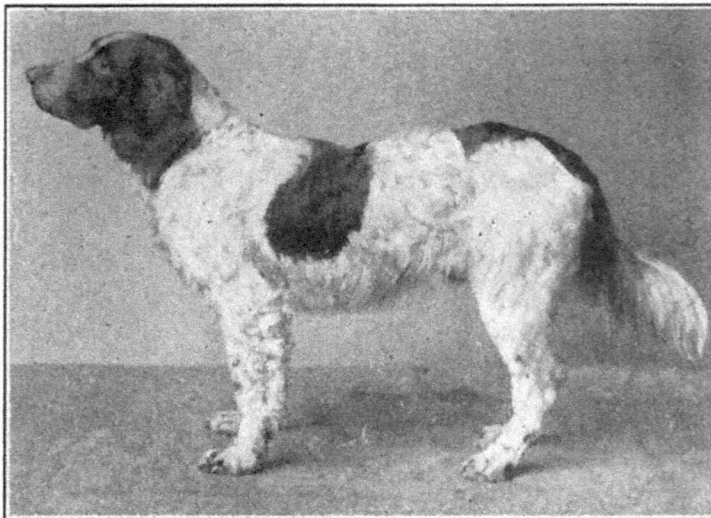

WACHTEL-HUND

Color: Self-colored brown, often with a white patch on stern and chest; white with large or small brown patches, or mixed.
Height: 20 in.
Weight: 56 lbs.

The Wachtelhund is somewhat like the German Setter in miniature and is strongly built, notwithstanding his small size. The head is large and long, skull slightly rounded and fairly broad. Muzzle of fair length and narrow with the occipital bone and stop both well defined. The eyes are dark in color, varying in shade with that of the coat and of medium size. The ears are long compared with those of the German Setter, are set on high and hang close to the head. The neck should be strong and not throaty; chest deep, back straight, broad and muscular, and the loins short and broad. He is strong and straight on the leg and the tail is usually docked and well feathered. The coat is slightly wavy, fairly long and very dense.

[70]

GRIFFON-KORTHALS

Color: Steel gray with brown patches or self-colored brown often mixed with grey hairs. Also white, grey with brown, or grey with yellow patches.
Height: 24 in.
Weight: 56 lbs.

This dog is of medium size, symmetrical and well built. The head is heavy and long, covered with wiry hair not too long, but there should be a good moustache and eyebrows. The muzzle is long and square, nasal bone convex and the stop not too abrupt. The eyes are large, very intelligent in expression and brown or dark yellow in color. The nose is always brown. Ears of medium size, set on not too low, carried close to the head. The back strong and well developed and the forelegs straight, muscular and covered with wiry hair. The stern is carried straight out and is covered with wiry hair but without feather. About a third of the stern is generally docked. The coat is wiry, crisp and harsh like fine iron wire, never curly or woolly. Undercoat is dense and soft.

BOXER

Color: Yellow or brindle, with or without black muzzle. White patches allowed, but liver color is a disqualification.
Height: 21 in.
Weight: 50 lbs.

A strong, lively, smooth-coated dog of great activity. The ears are set on high, are always cropped and when at attention the skull is freely wrinkled. The eyes are dark and large and his back is short and straight with well rounded ribs. The tail set high and is always docked. Coat short, hard and glossy.

HANOVRIAN LIMER

Color: Gray-brown, like the winter coat of a deer, tan, red-yellow, darker on the mask, ears, and around the eyes, and often with a dark trace down the back.
Height: 20 in. Weight: 54 lbs.

In general appearance this dog is of medium height, of strong and long structure. He is broad in skull and slightly domed, forehead slightly wrinkled, eyebrows well developed and protruding. The eyes show no haw and convey an energetic and earnest expression. Ears are very broad, set on high, and are carried close to the head. Chest wide and deep, back long with broad loins. The tail is long, strong at the root and tapering, well provided with long hair and carried downwards. The coat is close, full, smooth and elastic, and of a dull appearance.

BAVARIAN LIMER

Color: Tan, red-yellow, or wheaten, often darker on the back, with muzzle and ears nearly always black. Height: 20 in. Weight: 52 lbs.

A medium-sized dog, light in bone, with a grave and mild expression. Has a broad skull, slightly domed, eyebrows well developed, "stop" slightly defined, and lips not too heavy or pendulous. The eyes are dark brown and the haw is not visible. The ears are of medium length, broad, set on high, and round at the tips. Body not too long and chest fairly broad. Tail of good length, well covered with long hair, carried downwards, and is never docked. The coat is full and dense of hard texture, finer on the head and ears.

Italian Breeds

ITALIAN GREYHOUND   BOLOGNESE
ITALIAN GRIFFON   ITALIAN SHEEPDOG
ITALIAN POINTER   SHEEPDOG OF ABRUZZES

ITALIAN SHEEPDOG

Color: Dirty yellow, dark shades are not desirable.
Height: 23 in.
Weight: 62 lbs.
This is a strong, thick-set dog with heavy, somewhat rounded skull. The eyes are hazel color of intelligent expression. Ears are short and hanging, covered with fairly long, straight fur. His back is strong and straight; tail long, carried low and well coated, and the coat is curly and dense, except on the head, where it should be smooth.

SHEEPDOG OF THE ABRUZZES

Color: All white.
Height: 27 in.
Weight: 66 lbs.
A large and coarse dog. The head is fairly long, somewhat broad in skull, slightly domed, and without stop. The eyes are small and dark in color; ears of medium size and carried close to the head. Body strong and well built, with well developed and muscular loins. The tail is long, well coated, generally carried low, but sometimes over the back. His coat is dense and long, especially around the neck, on the back and on the tail. The skull, muzzle, ears and forepart of the legs are smooth coated. A curly coat is a serious fault.

ITALIAN GREYHOUND

Color: Self-colored, golden fawn, but all shades of fawn, red, mouse, blue, green, and white are recognized. Blacks, brindles and pied are less desirable.

Weight, two classes: Over 8 lbs. and under 8 lbs.

This is an English greyhound in miniature, of very slender proportions, and of ideal elegance and grace in shape, symmetry and action.

ITALIAN GRIFFON

Color: All white or white with yellow or light brown patches.
Height: 26 in. Weight: 56 lbs.

This dog is known as the Spinone and is a well-built and clever dog of medium size. The head is rather long and large and though the moustaches are abundant the rest of the hair on the head is of a smooth nature. The skull is not too broad, forehead slightly domed, muzzle square and long, and the stop not very clearly defined. The eyes, though yellow or light brown in color, are very intelligent. Ears not too large, set on rather high and hang close to the cheeks. The stern is carried straight or slightly upwards, and is generally docked. The coat is short, hard and wiry, never woolly or curly and the undercoat is dense.

ITALIAN POINTER

Color: White with orange patches, white speckled with lemon, white and liver, and roan with liver. Height: 25 in. Weight: 80 lbs.

The Italian Pointer is a strong, muscular and elegantly shaped dog, full of character. The skull is slightly rounded, occipital bone well developed with broad, long and straight muzzle. The eyes are oval in shape, dark yellow in color, sympathetic and grave in expression. The nose is of brown or flesh color, never black. The lips are pendulous, thick and rounded. Ears long and broad, set on at the height of the eye, hanging gracefully and round at the tips. The back and loins are broad and muscular. The stern is thick and tapering and is generally docked to about 7 in. in length.

BOLOGNESE

Color: Self-colored white.
Height: 12 in. or under.
Weight: 8 lbs. or less.

This is a ladies' toy dog. The head is rather broad and muzzle not too long. The eyes are large, dark in color and watery. The ears hang, but not too close to the head, which gives the head a square appearance, and are well covered with long, curly hair. He is straight in the back and deep in the chest. The tail is curled over the back and well coated, and his coat should be long, silky and curly.

Netherlands Breeds

DRAUGHT DOG   SCHIPPERKE (Belgium)
BRUSSELS GRIFFON (Belgium)   PAPILLON (Belgium)
TOY BRABANTINE (Belgium)   WIRE-HAIRED DUTCH TERRIER (Holland)
BELGIAN SHEEPDOG (Belgium)   DUTCH SHEEPDOG (Holland)
                    DANISH POINTER (Denmark)

DRAUGHT DOG

This is more or less of a nondescript variety, but he is worthy of a place in the sun by reason of the inestimable service he renders to his master or mistress. Daily he may be seen in Belgium and Holland drawing the carts purveying milk, butter, vegetables and other similar household necessities. He varies in height from about 24 in. to 32 in. and weighs around 100 lbs. Fawns and brindles are the most common colors. In general appearance he is a cobbily-built strong dog capable of great endurance. Naturally he must be strongly made in back and loins, well boned in legs and with feet well padded. The tail is generally docked to about three inches. Chapters dealing with other purposes to which dogs are put will be found in other parts of this work.

BRUSSELS GRIFFON

Color: Red.
Weight: Under 9 lbs.

This is a ladies' pet dog, very intelligent, sprightly, robust, of compact appearance, and is peculiar for his quasi-human expression. His head is rounded, furnished with hard, irregular hair, which is longer around the eyes and on the nose and cheeks. The ears are erect when cropped, but not otherwise. The eyes are very large, black and with long and black eye lashes, and the hair on his nose should grow upwards, towards his pronounced stop. His chin should be prominent, but must not show the teeth. The tail is erect and cut two-thirds of its length.

There is no definite data as to this dog's precise origin, and though credit for his conception belongs to Brussels, it is highly probable that he has been evolved by an admixture of the Yorkshire Terrier, Irish Terrier and the Ruby Spaniel. His quaintness and degree of dignity, altogether disproportionate to his size, account in a large measure for the popular esteem in which he is held.

TOY BRABANTINE

The Toy Branbantine resembles the Brussels Griffon in every respect, except that his coat is short and smooth and his color red, or black and tan.

[77]

BELGIAN SHEEPDOG

Color: Reddish-black, if possible with black muzzle. Height: 21 in. Weight: 54 lbs.

A very intelligent and rustic dog built to withstand the changeable climate of Belgium. His sagacity, activity and enduring strength and dauntless courage fit him peculiarly as a protector for his Belgian master. The head is long, skull flat, not too broad, and moderate "stop." The eyes are brown, with an inquiring intelligent expression. The ears should be stiff and carried erect, and triangular in shape, neck rather long, chest broad and not too deep, back straight, broad, strong, and of medium length. The tail is carried low in repose and should never be curled over the back, and is never docked. There are three varieties as to coat: A. Long and straight on the body, smooth on the head, with the inside of the ears protected by dense hair, and with considerable coat round the frill or mane. Forelegs well feathered and very profuse tail. B. Smooth on the body, head and legs, little longer round the neck, and slight feathering on the tail. C. A hard, dry and bristling wire-coat of the stand-off variety, more or less the same length all over the body, and with a bushy tail.

SCHIPPERKE

Color: All black.
Height: 12 in.
Weight: 12 lbs.

This is an excellent little watch dog, very active and always on the alert, very courageous, exceedingly inquisitive, and a good vermin dog. The head is foxy, eyes dark brown, oval, and keen. Ears quite erect, small, triangular and set on high, and very mobile. The body is short and thick-set, chest broad, with straight back and powerful loins. He has no tail. His coat should be dense and harsh on the body, very profuse around the neck, forming a mane and frill, but short and smooth on the ears and head.

[78]

PAPILLON

Color: Self-colored red mahogany, ruby, chestnut red, dark yellow, or white with these patches. Height: Not more than 10 in., the smaller the better. Weight: 8 lbs. and under.

This is a lively and active ladies' pet dog. The skull is small, slightly domed, and muzzle rather snipy. The eyes are round, dark colored, set low in the head, and convey a lively expression. The ears are set high on the head, carried erect like the wings of a butterfly, from which feature he is often styled the Butterfly Spaniel. The back is straight and not too short or cobby. The tail is carried like that of the squirrel and is long and heavily feathered, which again accounts for him sometimes being called the Squirrel Spaniel. His coat should be long and silky, abundant on the body and tail and ears, but short on the mask.

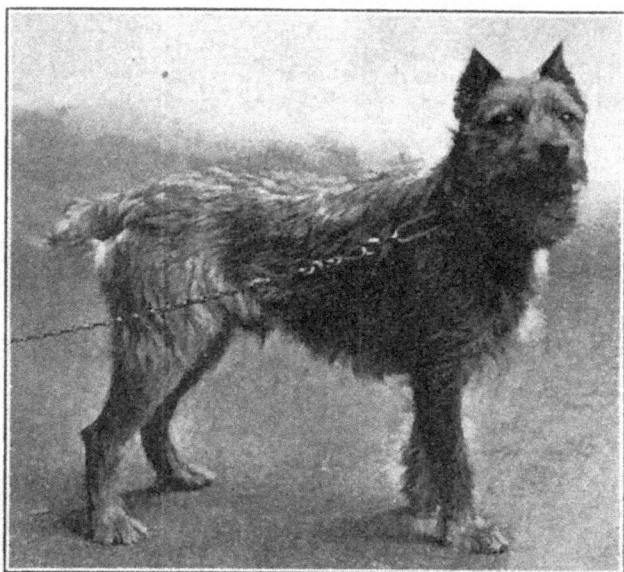

WIRE HAIRED DUTCH TERRIER

Color: Red, yellow-brown, dirty yellow with moustaches, beard and eye lashes often black. Height: 17 in. Weight: 27 lbs.

This is a rather commonly built dog, lively and intelligent; is a good ratter and is a stable dog rather than a ladies' pet. The head is rather round and short, with stop well defined and the skull well covered with a short and hard coat. The eyes are rather large and round, dark brown in color, with an intelligent and lively expression. The ears are set on high, carried erect, and cropped to points, covered with coat shorter and softer than on the body. The tail is always docked, carried gaily and should be well coated but without feathering. The coat is hard, wiry and rough, never curly, wavy or woolly.

[79]

DUTCH SHEEPDOG

Color: Immaterial, but no pie colors allowed. Height: 21 in. Weight: 52 lbs.

A strong, well-built dog, very active and intelligent. The head is rather long and narrow, with flat skull, no stop, ears erect and of medium size, pointed at the tip and set on high. The neck is muscular and clean. Chest deep but not too broad, back strong, and on the short side. The tail is carried low, and is never docked. There are three varieties as to coat.

A. A short, smooth coat like that of the smooth collie; B. A long, rough coat similar to the rough collie but without the frill; C. A wiry or broken coat with smooth mask, and with distinct beard and eyebrows.

DANISH POINTER

Color: Yellow-orange with white markings on the legs, feet, chest, muzzle and tip of tail. Self-colored yellow-orange is objectionable.

Height: 26 in. Weight: 60 lbs.

In general appearance the Danish Pointer is smaller in size than the other varieties;

the head is light and fairly long, muzzle long and broad; eyes of medium size and brown topaz in color, giving a pleasant expression, ears soft and hanging gracefully close to the cheeks and moderately long; neck is long, round and arched, free from dewlaps; body though light is powerful looking; back not too short and very strong, with loins and hindquarters full of muscle; stern fine and rather short.

Austro-Hungarian Breeds

AUSTRIAN HOUND   BOSNIAN HOUND
HUNGARIAN SHEEPDOG   DALMATIAN

AUSTRIAN HOUND

Color: Black with tan or yellow, brown and red in all shades and self-colored white.
Height: 21 in.
Weight: About 50 lbs.

A dog of medium size, rather long, strong and of elastic structure. The head is of medium size, broad in skull, eyebrows well defined, and with pendulous lips. Eyes bright, brown and intelligent. Ears of medium length, not too broad, round at the tips, and set high. The body is strong, neck of medium length and very strong, chest broad and fairly long in the back. Stern is long, strong at the root and tapering. The coat: A, smooth, dense and glossy; B, semi-long, wiry and dull.

HUNGARIAN SHEEPDOG

Color: White or dirty white, sometimes seen with a yellow tip on the ears.
Height: 27 in.
Weight: 73 lbs.
This is a well-made muscular dog, with broad skull, long and tapering muzzle. The eyes are small, set in obliquely and rather close together, of dark color and of an energetic and sometimes sour expression. The ears are small and carried close to the head and covered with smooth hair. The back is long, straight and well developed.

The tail is carried low. His coat is fairly long, flat, dense and hard, sometimes wavy, but never curly.

BOS-
NIAN
HOUND

Color: Red, brown white, yellow, or red patches and tri-color. Height: 25 in.
Weight: 65 lbs.

This is a well-built, lively dog and conveys the impression of great stamina. The
head is somewhat like that of the rough-coated German pointer, eyes bright, yellow or
light brown in color, and of medium size. His heavy eyebrows give a rather threaten-
ing expression. Ears of medium length, broad, rounded at the tips, set on high, and
hanging close to the head. He is broad in chest with neck long and well arched and
well rounded in rib. Stern of fair length, strong at the root and carried downwards.
The coat is hard, wiry and dense.

DALMA-
TIAN

Color: Color together with markings are most important. The ground should be
white. He should be spotted with either black or liver-colored spots clearly defined
and on no account should the spots run into each other and they should be as round
as possible. Height: 22 in. Weight: 55 lbs.

A strong, muscular, active dog capable of great endurance. In size, build and
outline he very much resembles the pointer.

The eyes are round, bright and sparkling, as dark as possible in the black spotted
dogs, though a yellow tint is allowed in the liver dogs. Ears are set on high, of
moderate size and carried close to the head, of fine texture, and the more profusely
they are spotted the better. His back is strong and muscular, tail of fair length carried
with a nice curve upwards but not curled and should be well spotted. The coat is
short, hard, dense and fine in texture, but must not be woolly or silky.

[82]

Spanish Breeds

SPANISH POINTER

Color: Brown and white, red and white, black and white, and pure brown. The white must not predominate.
Height: 24 in.
Weight: 80 lbs.

In general appearance the Spanish Pointer is a somewhat heavy, loosely made dog, larger than the English Pointer. The head is indented between the eyes, broad in skull, square, long and broad in muzzle with lips large and pendulous. The eyes are large and somewhat sunken in the head. Ears thin, loose and of moderate length. Chest broad and deep. Back and hind quarters very muscular. The stern is strong at the root, tapering towards the end and is frequently docked.

MEDELAN

Color: A dirty color or grizzled red with white patches and always shaded with black or darker color, like the St. Bernard and Mastiff.
Height: 27 in.
Weight: 180 lbs.

A powerful and imposing dog resembling in many features the Mastiff and the Bordeaux, but is longer and harder in coat. The head is very heavy, powerful, large and square, with skull broad between the ears. The muzzle short, blunt, broad and square, and the lips have heavy pendulous flews. Eyes are small and brown, and convey a grave and sometimes an almost grumbling expression, and show the haw. Ears small, set on high, and hang close to the head. Body is strong, neck strong, heavy and muscular, chest deep and broad, back long, broad and powerful. Tail long, heavy, and carried downwards. Coat is semi-long, dense and hard.

Swiss Breeds

St. Bernard	Lucern Hound
Swiss Setter	Bern Hound
	Swiss Hound

ST. BERNARD

Color: Red, orange, various shades of brindle, or white with patches on body, of the above named colors. He should have white muzzle, blaze up face, collar, chest, forelegs, feet and end of tail, with black shadings on face and ears.

Height: Not less than 30 in.

Weight: 200 lbs.

This dog is known as the "Saintly" breed and may by his size, magnificent appearance, beautiful temper and docility be justly regarded as one of the finest examples and most noble members of the canine species. The head is large and massive, short and square in the muzzle, with great depth from eye to lower jaw. The eyes are rather small, deeply set and dark in color, the lower eyelid drooping, showing the haw. His expression should betoken benevolence, dignity and intelligence. Ears of medium size and not heavily feathered. Chest wide and deep with level back, well rounded ribs, and very muscular loins. He should be strong and straight on his legs. The tail is long and bushy, carried low when in repose. There are two varieties as regards coat: A. In the long-coated variety it should be dense and flat, rather fuller around the neck, with the thighs well feathered; B. In the short-coated variety, it should be close and hound-like and only slightly feathered on thighs and tail.

SWISS SETTER

Color: Mixed chestnut and grizzle, trout color, or white and chestnut with grizzled patches. Height: 24 in. Weight: 52 lbs.

In general appearance the Swiss Setter is a well built, intelligent and rustic looking dog. The head is rather light and short skull round and broad, occipital bone well developed, and with a well defined stop. The eyes should not be too small and should be brown or yellow brown in color. Back straight, strong and muscular, chest well developed, but not too broad, and well rounded in rib. The stern is often docked, otherwise it should be carried scimitar shaped. The coat should be very dense, but not hard.

LUCERN HOUND

Color: Iron-gray, steel-blue, blue mottled with large dark or black patches, and some have the head, body and paws with pale yellow or tan markings. Height: 19 in. Weight: 45 lbs.

A dog of medium size and of fine structure. Head long, narrow and fine, eyes bright, large and intelligent, and dark brown in color, ears set on low, not too broad, are long and carried close to the head, with rounded tips. He is straight and broad in back. Stern of medium length and tapering to a point. The coat is short, smooth, fine and glossy.

BERN HOUND

Color: Tri-color, white, black, brown-yellow, or tan. White with large black patches and tan markings on the eyes, jaws, and inside of the ears.

Height: 21 in.

Weight: 50 lbs.

This is a leggy and longish dog of elegant and muscular build. The head is long, narrow and somewhat pinched. Skull high and occipital bone well developed. The eyes are bright and dark. Ears set on backwards and are long but not too broad. They are rather pointed at the tips. Is deep and broad in chest, long and not too broad in back. Stern is not too heavy, tapers to the point and is carried down. He is smooth, short and fine in coat.

SWISS HOUND

Color: White w i t h large yellow, orange or tan patches. Frequently spotted with red or yellow markings and a black shade with red color is permissible. The skin is often spotted with black, giving him a blue appearance when out of coat.

Height: 20 in.

Weight: 46 lbs.

A dog of medium size, strong but not heavily built. The skull is broad and the occipital bone well developed, eyes rather large but not prominent, hazel brown, bright and intelligent. The ears are not set on too high, are thin and moderately long, and covered with fine hair. Chest deep and not too broad, and is short and broad in back. Stern of medium length, fairly short, strong at the root, and well coated. There are two varieties as to coat: A. Smooth and dense, which is fine and glossy on the head, ears and shoulders, and coarser on the back; B. Medium length, coarse, hard and dull.

Russian Breeds

BORZOI (Russian Wolfhound)   RUSSIAN HOUND
RUSSIAN YELLOW RETRIEVER   OWTCHAR
SAMOYED

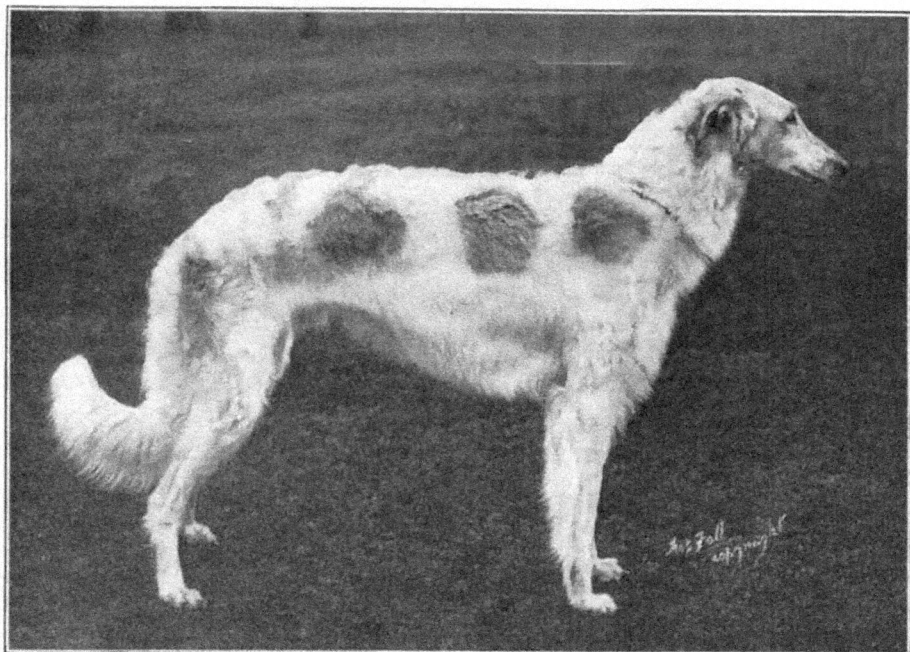

BORZOI

Color: Immaterial, except that self-colored specimens or those with heavy, black markings are objectionable.
Height: 33 in.
Weight: 100 lbs.
The Borzoi is one of the most ancient of Russian breeds and should possess great size, great speed and great strength. The head is of extraordinary length, and should appear rather Roman nosed in profile. The eyes are dark, expressive and almond shaped; ears small, thin and placed well back on the head; the chest is deep and narrow; the back bony, and well arched; loins broad and very powerful, with well sprung ribs; the tail is long and well feathered and carried low; the coat should be long and silky, not woolly, and on the neck it should be profuse and rather curly.
This breed, though originating from Russia, has been bred and exhibited in England since 1872. The Duchess of Newcastle and, a little later, Queen Alexandra, then the Princess of Wales, are mainly responsible for the popular favor in which they are now regarded. The finest collection in the world, however, is owned by the Grand Duke Nicholas, at Perchina, near Moscow. These are said to excel even th se possessed by the Czar, from whom dogs cannot be purchased.

RUSSIAN YELLOW RETRIEVERS

Color: Yellow or rich red sable. Height: 28 in. Weight: 90 lbs.

This dog is similar in all essentials to the English Retriever, except that he is a size bigger and heavier in coat, and of course different in color, as his name implies. He is used principally for tracking wounded deer.

RUSSIAN HOUND

Color: Grizzle or black, with tan markings, often with a white collar, feet and tip of tail. Height: 20 in. Weight: 58 lbs.

The head much resembles that of a wolf, being considerably broader between the ears than at the forehead. Eyes of medium size, bright, brown or yellow, sometimes nearly black. Ears small and hanging with a tendency to prick when the dog is angry. Stern is short, strong at the root, and carried straight. The coat is hard and smooth, with a woolly under coat, and the wolf or fox brush.

OWTCHAR (Russian Sheepdog)

Color: Slate color, dirty white, and nearly black. Height: 32 in. Weight: 105 lbs. This is a large and strongly built dog of very great antiquity. His head is massive, round, and covered with softer hair than on the body. The eyes are rather large, dark brown in color, and very intelligent. The ears are of fair size, hanging, well coated, and are sometimes cut and carried semi-erect. He has a short, muscular neck, strong, well developed body, and is the largest of all the varieties of the sheep dogs, and is intended to defend his flocks against wolves. The tail is often docked, otherwise it should be well coated, and his coat is very dense and somewhat woolly.

SAMOYED

Color: White or white with black, brown or wolf patches.

Height: 22 in.
Weight: 65 lbs.

A dog of medium size, well built and cobby, covered with a thick fur. The head is slightly domed and fairly broad. He is rather small in eyes, which should be dark in color and set obliquely in the head, and convey a very intelligent and lively expression. The ears are erect, broad at the root, and taper to a point. The neck is strong and muscular, the chest broad and deep, and back short, straight and strong. Tail is short and heavily coated, and carried curled over the back. His stand-off coat is semi-long, dense and thick, and abundant around the neck, with a short and dense undercoat.

Breeds of the Northern Latitudes of Europe and Asia

FINNISH POM
FINNISH ELKHOUND
NORWEGIAN ELKHOUND
SWEDIAN HOUND

NORWEGIAN HOUND
ICELAND DOG
DOG OF NOORLAND
LAPLAND SHEEPDOG

ESQUIMAU

Dogs Sledging in the Icefields of the Northern Latitudes.

FINNISH POM

Color: Foxy-red or yellow-red, often with a white patch on chest, feet and tip of tail.

Height: 18 in.
Weight: 56 lbs.

A cobbily-built dog with an intrepid and audacious appearance. The head of medium size, lean, not too round, and stop well defined. Eyes are obliquely set in the head, giving him a mild, lively and intelligent expression, and are dark or light brown in color. The ears are set on high, carried erect, very mobile, and of moderate size. Has muscular neck, chest deep but not too broad, and body straight, broad and short. The tail is thick at the root, profusely covered with long hair, and carried curled over the back. His coat is smooth on head and forelegs, but long, dense and perfectly straight on the body with a dense and fluffy undercoat. It should be very abundant around the neck, forming a frill.

FINNISH HOUND

Color: Red-brown, shade of yellow on muzzle and legs; white patches permissible.

Height: 23 in.

Weight: 65 lbs.

A proportionately built dog with long, broad muzzle, light brown eyes, deep chest, muscular loins, rather high on leg in proportion to his body, medium length tail, carried like a saber. His coat is flat, smooth though rather coarse on the back.

NORWEGIAN ELKHOUND

Color: Grizzle in all its shade: g r i z z l e - brown, grizzle - brown and black. A white patch on the chest and feet is permissible. The undercoat should be pale brown.

Height: 20 in.

Weight: 60 lbs.

In stature this dog is rather short, but he has much strength and temerity. The head is carried high, is large and square, broad between the ears, with "stop" well defined. Eyes should be dark brown or yellow-brown and convey an active and courageous expression. The ears are pointed, carried erect and very mobile. The body is short, and the chest broad and deep. The stern is of medium length, thick and heavy and carried curled over the back. His coat is short and flat on the head but hard, coarse and rather long on the body.

[91]

SWEDIAN
HOUND

Color: Black—the head, chest and legs being tan or dark yellow. White patches on the head, chest, feet and tip of tail are permissible. Also tan or dark yellow with large white patches. Height: 33 in. Weight: 65 lbs.

This is a well-built dog with a noble head, which is long and lean. The eyes are bright and for preference are dark in color. Chest deep and straight and broad in the back. Stern of medium length, strong at the root, and carried with a slight curve. His coat is thick, hard, dense and glossy.

NORWEGIAN HOUND

Color: Iron gray patches and spots on blue background; so-called "trout" color with brown-brindle in patches, tan markings; blue-merle; black with tan or brown markings; tan with white patches. Iron-gray with tan markings is not desirable. Height: 20 in. Weight: 60 lbs.

This is a strongly built dog rather long in body, and with a grave and intelligent expression. The head is large, of medium breadth, not domed and with distinct "stop." Eyes are brown. Blue-merle dogs have "China" ears. Ears set on rather high, of medium length and breadth, and hang close to the head. The chest is broad rather than deep. Stern of medium length, carried rather high. The coat is thick and glossy.

ICELAND DOG

Color: Brownish or gray, sometimes dirty white or dirty yellow, and is frequently seen with black on the back.

Height: 14 in.

Weight: 45 lbs.

This is a lightly built dog with a "game" temperament. The head is large in proportion to his body, with broad domed skull, and rather short, snipy muzzle. The ears are large at the base, pointed and carried erect, though sometimes semi-erect. He is large and deep in chest, short in body, with bushy tail carried over the back. His coat is hard, of medium length, flat and shorter on the head and legs.

DOG OF NOORLAND

Color: All shades of grizzle with black or darker tips. The under coat should be as white as possible. A yellow undercoat is a fault.

Height: 22 in.

Weight: 65 lbs.

A strong and well-built dog on rather cobby lines; the head is rather small, slightly arched and without "stop." Eyes should be dark brown, bright and intelligent. Ears small, very mobile, carried erect and set high on the head. Chest deep and broad. The tail is strong, medium length, and curled over the back. The coat is short and thick on the head, legs and feet, and more abundant on the body.

LAPLAND SHEEPDOG

Color: Black, rusty black, grizzle with white feet. White dogs with reddish brown patches and self-colored yellow-brown ones are highly appreciated, but all white is a fault.

Height: 20 in.

Weight: 56 lbs

This dog has a rather long body, which is well covered with thick, abundant coat. The skull is broad and domed; ears erect; eyes large, brown and intelligent; chest narrow and deep. His tail is sometimes docked, but when not is well coated and curled over the back. The coat on the head is short, but on the body should be long, thick and dense, and never wavy, and he should have a very dense undercoat and a distinct frill.

ESQUIMAU

Color: Black or rusty black with white patches, and white chest. Sometimes brown with gray patches and all white. Height: 16 in. Weight: 56 lbs.

This is a medium-sized, well-boned dog, with broad domed skull, rather snipy muzzle, with well defined "stop." The ears are broad, pointed and carried erect, and the insides should be well coated. The eyes are small, dark in color, and of intelligent expression. The chest is broad rather than deep and the tail long, bushy and carried over the back. His coat is dense, flat, hard and long, especially on the back, with dense, woolly undercoat.

[94]

United States of America Breeds

BOSTON TERRIER   CHESAPEAKE

AMERICAN BLOODHOUND   AMERICAN FOXHOUND

BOSTON TERRIER

Color: Brindle with even white markings. Weight: Not exceeding 27 lbs., divided into three classes, as follows: A, under 17 lbs.; B, 17 to 22 lbs.; C, 22 to 27 lbs.

The general appearance of the Boston Terrier should be that of a lively, highly intelligent, smooth coated, short headed, compactly built, short tailed, well balanced dog. The head should indicate a high degree of intelligence, the body rather short and well knit, limbs strong a n d neatly turned. This dog should convey an appearance of determination, strength and activity, with easy, graceful carriage. Color and even white markings are given particular consideration in the matter of general appearance. The skull is square, flat, free from wrinkles, abrupt brow, eyes wide apart, large and round, and dark in color. The muzzle is short, square, wide and deep, and free from wrinkles, and the ears should be small and thin. The body is deep with wide chest, and well sprung ribs. The tail is set on low, straight or screw, short, fine and tapering, and the coat is short, smooth and of fine texture.

AMERICAN BLOODHOUND

Color: Tan, black and tan. The black and tan must be well defined; white is not allowed except a small spot on the breast. Height: 28 in. Weight: 60 lbs.

A dog showing much hound character, but is smaller and lighter in muzzle and bone than the English Bloodhound. The skull should be rounded crossways with the occiput slightly prominent. The eyes are piercing with hound expression and hazel in color. The ears should reach to end of muzzle and as much longer as possible; they are thin, covered with a soft silky coat, and low set. The neck should be clean and of good length without throatiness. Back broad, strong and short and hind quarters very strong and muscular. The stern is not very strong in bone at the root and of medium length. The coat is not rough, nor so fine as to be silky, wiry or shaggy.

[95]

CHESAPEAKE

Color: Nearly resembling wet sedge grass or discolored coat of the Buffalo. Height: 24 in. Weight: 65 lbs.

A symmetrical and well built dog with a head somewhat broad, yellow eyes, small ears placed well upon the head, of lively and intelligent expression. Powerfully built, with a somewhat coarse coat which has a tendency to waviness over the shoulders. His skin is protected from the water by a short woolly and dense undercoat.

AMERICAN FOXHOUND

Color: Not material, but usually black and tan and white. Height: Males, 24 in. Weight: 60 lbs.

The American Foxhound is a strong, clean-limbed dog, built on lighter lines than his English brother and resembles him in all other essentials.

[96]

Mexican Breeds

MEXICAN
HAIRLESS

Color: Generally color of elephant's hide. The skin always feels cold and is often mottled with flesh-colored, pink or grizzle patches. Weight: From 8 to 20 lbs.

In body properties they somewhat resemble the black and tan "Manchester" terrier. The "points" of this breed are not sufficiently well known to have enabled breeders to formulate a standard.

CHIHUAHUA

Color: Reddish black and fawn. Weight: From 1½ to 4 lbs.

This dog is strictly of Mexican origin, though it is also found in the state of Texas. It is the most diminutive of all breeds. Is remarkably game and exclusive in its affections. His legs are very slender and toe nails very long and strong, features which seem to justify the belief that in early days they inhabited the dense forests of northern Mexico. The head is round with sharp pointed nose, and large erect ears.

This breed is famous as a performing dog, being very intelligent and agile.

[97]

Japanese Breed

JAPANESE SPANIEL

JAPANESE SPANIEL

Color: Black and white, or red and white. The term red includes all shades of sable, brindle, lemon and orange, but the brighter and clearer the red the better. The white should be clear white and whatever color the patches are they should be evenly distributed over the body, cheeks and ears.

This is a lively, highly bred little dog, of dainty, smart appearance, compact carriage, profuse coat, and very stylish in movement. The head should be large, broad, and slightly rounded, with strong and wide muzzle, very short from eyes to nose. The under-jaw should be slightly turned up, but the teeth should not be shown. The nose should be wide and open, and must be the color of the dog's markings. The eyes are large, dark, lustrous, prominent and set wide apart. Ears small, nicely feathered and set high on the head. The body is very compact and squarely built with short cobby back. In fact the length of the dog should be about equal to his total height. The tail is carried in a tight curl over the back and should be profusely feathered, so as to give the appearance of a beautiful plume.

During the last thirty years the popular taste for the Japanese Spaniel has called for smaller and smaller specimens, until now the more diminutive they are the more valuable have they become. In Japan they are affected by the ladies as "sleeve" dogs, such being almost priceless. It is not now uncommon to find them 2½ lbs. weight, though fully matured. These small specimens are now also freely bred in England, the climate of which country appears to suit them very well.

Chinese Breeds

Pekingese Spaniel
Happa
Chow-Chow

Pug
Chinese Crested
Little Lion Dog

PEKINGESE

Color: All colors are allowable—red, fawn, black, black and tan, sable, brindle, white and parti colors. Those with black masks and "spectacles" around the eyes and lines to ears are the most appreciated.

Weight: A. 10 to 18 lbs.; B. Under 10 lbs.

This is probably the most fashionable pet dog now in vogue. His character is full of dignity and consummate pride, and disgust for anything menial or common. His head is massive, broad, wide and flat between the ears and eyes. The eyes should be large, dark, prominent, round and lustrous. "Stop" deep. Ears heart-shaped, drooping and well feathered. Muzzle very short, broad and wrinkled. He has a heavy-fronted body and light hind quarters, and the great coat on the frill and neck give him a lion-like appearance. The coat should be long, straight and flat, with dense under-coat and well feathered on thighs, legs, tail and toes.

HAPPA

The Happa is identical in every respect with the Pekingese Spaniel, except that his coat is short and smooth.

CHOW-CHOW

Colors: Black, red, yellow, blue, white. All self-colors. Height: 20 in. Weight: 50 lbs.

A lively, compact, short-bodied dog with well-knit frame, and tail curled well over the back. The skull is flat and broad, well filled out under the eyes, and broad at the snout. His tongue should be black, eyes dark and small, though in the blue shades a lighter colored eye is permissible. The ears are small, pointed and erect, and should be placed well forward over the eyes, a feature which gives the dog a characteristic expression or "scowl" peculiar to the breed. The chest is broad and deep; back short, straight and strong, and his coat in the rough variety should be abundant, dense, straight, coarse in texture, with a soft woolly undercoat. Smooth-coated CHOWS are identically the same as above, except that the coat should be smooth, short and dense.

PUG

Color: Silver fawn, apricot fawn, black.
Height: 12 in.
Weight: 17 lbs.

This is a square and cobby dog, short in body, and wide in chest. His compactness of form and hardness of developed muscle are his chief characteristics. The head is large, massive and round, muzzle short, blunt and square, and he should have large and deep wrinkles. The eyes are very large, dark, bold and prominent, with a soft and solicitous expression, and when excited be full of "fire." The ears are thin, small and soft and of two varieties as regards carriage—"rose" and "button." The tail is curled as tightly as possible over the hip; a double curl is considered perfection. His coat is fine, smooth, soft short and glossy, neither too hard nor too woolly.

CHINESE CRESTED DOG

Height: 12 in.
Weight: 20 lbs.
This is a hairless breed, except that he has a silky top-knot or crest, and some feathering or tuft at the root of the tail, which feature is considered very typical of the breed. It is difficult to assign its origin, but they are found freely in the South and Central American States, Mexico, South Africa and China. The ears should be carried erect and are never cut. The conformation of the body is like that of the black and tan terrier, but the head is shorter and the skull more rounded. The skin always feels cold and is of the color of the hide of an elephant. Some are mottled with flesh colored patches, and sometimes the skin is of a pink color with grizzle patches.

LITTLE LION DOG

Color: All colors; self-colored or parti colors. The most preferable being the self-colored white, black and lemon.
Height: 14 in.
Weight: 9 lbs.
This is a small ladies' pet dog, very active and intelligent, generally with one-third of his body clipped or shaved, which gives him the appearance of a lion in miniature. The head is short and broad; eyes large, round and intelligent, and dark in color, and his well feathered ears are long and hanging. The tail is of medium length, is clipped at the root, and well feathered at the tip. The coat is long and wavy, but not curly.

[101]

Various Greyhounds

BALEARIC (Spain)   PERSIAN

PHU-QUOC (Siam)   PORTUGUESE

ARABIAN

In addition to the above named varieties of the Greyhound, there are others known as Greyhounds of Crimea, of Caucasus, of Circassia, of Tartary, of Kurdistan, and of Anatoly. None of these, however, have any adopted "points," but are rather the result of crossings between the Borzoi and the different Asiatic greyhounds which are portrayed in other parts of this work.

As a general rule these dogs are used for hunting various kinds of fleet-footed game, sometimes in the interest of sport, but more frequently in the protection of the homestead against wolves and other kinds of wild beasts.

BALEARIC GREYHOUND

Color: Red fawn or fawn with white patches.
Height: 25 in.
Weight: 66 lbs.

This is a lean-looking dog and by no means elegant. The skull is slightly domed, narrow and long, and the jaws are long and powerful. His almond-shaped, brown eyes convey a sour expression. The ears are pointed, erect, set on high, turned outwards, and very movable. The head is lean and straight, neck straight and rather short, with short and powerful loins. The coat is short, hard and fairly long on the back, neck and tail.

PHU-QUOC GREYHOUND

Color: Reddish-fawn with black muzzle and with dark strip down the back.
Height: 21 in. Weight: 40 lbs.

This is a heavy kind of greyhound with a long, slightly domed skull, broad muzzle, jaw is long and powerful, lips and tongue black and with reddish eyes giving him a savage expression. The ears are carried erect, shell shaped and somewhat pointed. He is coarse in body, very long and flexible in neck, with broad and strong loins. The tail is short, very movable and carried curled over the back. The coat on the body and legs is very short and dense, and this dog is peculiar and different from any other kind in that the hair on the back grows the wrong way, and is much longer and harder there than on the rest of his body.

PORTUGUESE GREYHOUND

Color: Reddish-roe, dark yellow, mouse grey, or black, with small white patch only on the chest. Height: 29 in. Weight About 56 lbs.

A muscular and well-built dog, but rather coarse for a greyhound. The head is narrow and pointed, jaws long, strong and powerful, and his hazel-brown eyes convey a lively expression. The ears are large, carried erect, sometimes semi-erect, pointed and set on not too high. The back is long and slightly arched, with muscular and rather coarse body, tail long and fine, carried upwards in a slight curve. Coat is smooth and in others wire-haired or broken.

[103]

PERSIAN GREYHOUND

Color: Black, various shades of fawn and sometimes a dirty white.
Height: 28 in.
Weight: 70 lbs.
This is a rather big dog, but delicate and elegant in outline. His head is fine, light, lean and bony, with a slightly domed skull. The eyes are mild, intelligent and dark brown. The ears hang close to the head, are long and well feathered with wavy hair. The neck is arched, elegant and slender. Chest deep and back straight, long and strong. He is moderately long in tail, which is carried hanging like a sabre. The coat is smooth and very soft, but is much longer on the ears and tail, where it is silky and wavy.

ARABIAN GREYHOUND

Color: Light yellow sand color with black mask and black eyelids.
Height: 28 in.
Weight: 65 lbs.
This is a dog of lean, elegant and alert appearance. He is higher on the leg and shorter in the body than the English Greyhound. He is not as long in the head but more domed in the skull than the English dog, and seen in profile the head has some resemblance to that of the Jackal. The eyes are large, dark amber in color, and intelligent in expression. He is rather large in ears, which are folded well down on the neck. He is strong and muscular in neck with hind quarters well developed. The tail is fairly long, fine and carried curved downwards. The coat is smooth, dense and fine.

[104]

Belgian Dogs trained to draw quick-firing guns

Dogs in Warfare

"Cry Havoc! and let slip the dogs of war"

HOWEVER trite may be the saying that history repeats itself, it is unquestionably apposite in regard to the employment of dogs in warfare. Great hounds were used to guard the camps of Rome. In even more primitive times they were formidable adversaries in hand-to-hand conflicts, while to come to more modern days Frederick the Great and Napoleon—two of the greatest soldiers the world has ever seen—held a very high opinion of the value of canine sentries. Napoleon, in fact, is said to have urged Marmont to fasten dogs to stakes around the circuit of the walls of Alexandria to keep guard.

Recent wars have served to emphasize the advantages which may be gained by the use of the peculiar qualities of scent and hearing which dogs possess. Their sense of scent we human beings lack almost entirely, while they not only hear audible things more quickly than we do, but also hear things which are quite inaudible to us. Is it to be wondered at, therefore, that military experts have not been slow to recognize such potential properties?

WHAT THEY HAVE DONE

The present-day tendency consequently is to bring dogs more and more into the foreground in warfare. During the Russo-Japanese War the whole of the Manchurian Railway line was guarded by dogs, who gave the alarm, and on several occasions prevented the Japanese crossing the line. Those which were sent out from England with the Abor Expedition, N. W. Frontier, more than once prevented the sentries from being rushed during night duty, owing to their keener sense of hearing. In the Tripoli campaign their value was frequently demonstrated, while the dogs belonging to Major Richardson, the famous English trainer of war dogs, rendered yeoman service to the Bulgarians at the siege of Adrianople, where they were able to give warning of attempted sorties by the Turks. Some of Major Richardson's well-trained animals were also used in the Spanish trenches in Morocco, being responsible for the finding of hundreds of wounded men who would otherwise have been left to their fate.

[105]

At the present moment most of the modern armies employ dogs, although naturally opinions differ as to the most suitable type of dog. The Russians have adopted the Caucasian dog, Austria, Dalmatians; Turkey, Asiatic Sheepdogs; France and Belgium, the smugglers' dogs of the Belgium frontier; while Germany uses Collies, Pointers and Airedales. So far the British Army has ignored the value of trained dogs, though the Admiralty some five years ago instituted a scheme for the use of dogs in naval stations ashore. Major Richardson believes that the only really useful dogs are the Airedale, Sheepdog, and Bloodhound.

What part dogs will play in the present great conflict time only will show, but that it will probably be a large one may be gathered from the fact that the German army alone possesses over 6,000.

Corps of Sentry Dogs

The importance of determining some efficient and economical form of traction for Infantry machine guns had been under consideration in Belgium before the war. Up till recently, pack-horse transport had been considered the most satisfactory system. Exhaustive trials between this method and that of wheel traction by a pair of dogs of a breed known in that country as the Belgian Mastiff, have, however, resulted in favour of the latter, and the final adoption of this mode of transport for the Machine Gun Units of the Belgium Army. This form of traction is not novel in Belgium in civil life. According to the Journal of the Royal Artillery the breeding of dogs for light draught purposes has long been in vogue in that country, for the purpose of conveying farm produce from the country into the towns. Dog traction is employed by the country people,—milkmen, bakers, greengrocers, and many artisans with light carts, in conducting their trade and business. There are reckoned to be 50,000 dogs available for this purpose in Belgium, of which 10,000 are in Brussels alone. They are found to be admirably suited for the purpose. Their bodies are thick set, loins strong, and they have deep chests, and muscular limbs. A dog of 110 lbs. weight is capable of drawing on a good road a load of 880 lbs., and a horse 1,100 to 1,300 lbs. (or ten times and upwards the weight of one of these dogs), cannot draw much more than the equivalent increase of his weight. With an average load of 660 lbs. behind the team on good roads, a dog can keep up for long distances a pace of 4 or 5 miles an hour; for several hundred yards he can attain a speed of from 6 to 7 miles an hour.

The price of a pack-horse is not less than £40, and his daily forage may be reckoned to cost about 1 / 4½ a day, without taking into consideration the construction and up-keep of his stable. The pack-saddle costs about £15, whereas dog harness can be pur-chased for the pair of dogs for something less than £4. A male dog costs £4, and his food per day amounts to about 4¼d. Finally, the small carriage for the machine gun or ammunition cart costs about £8, and the net cost for construction and upkeep of kennels is something small. Moreover, as the dog does not require shoes, lameness is rare, which we well know from the enormous distances he can go when hunting. He is intelligent and docile, and puts all his heart into serving his master faithfully under all circumstances. The length of his military service may be taken at from eight to nine years. The discipline of the trained dog is such that an untrained dog, harnessed with him, would be compelled to submit to all the movements of the former. On the march, and under fire, one can rely on his working till absolutely exhausted or mortally wounded. These are the qualities which can be developed in the breeding kennel, and in his subsequent training. The four wheels of the little gun carriage

[106]

are made of tubes of steel, light, low and stable, and fitted with pneumatic tires. The carriage complete does not weigh more than 220 lbs., and is easily dragged by the team of two dogs, or eventually carried by the four members of the detachment. Its height and breadth are each about 31 inches. The trials were carried out to test the following:—Visibility, mobility on roads and across country, overcoming obstacles, and resistance to fatigue. They lasted three weeks in bad weather, during which a distance of 250 miles was covered. The six pack-horses were wither-galled, and had to be successively replaced but not so the dogs. On the march across country, or commons, of from 1½ to 3 miles, where the ground presented obstacles or was broken up, the dogs gained without doubt in mobility and speed over the horses, especially when ditches, hedges and low walls had to be negotiated. The teams crossed with ease ploughed land and crops, copses and banks. Assisted by the detachments they crossed over deep ditches and steep slopes. The horses showed signs of fatigue long before the dogs. The latter were afraid of nothing, and followed perfectly the member of the detachment charged with leading each team. They lay down or resumed the order of march on a signal, without even barking, and in perfect order.

The smallest fold in the ground concealed the teams, and at 300 yards distance, nothing of them could be distinguished. Coming into or out of action was more rapidly effected than in the case of the pack-horses.

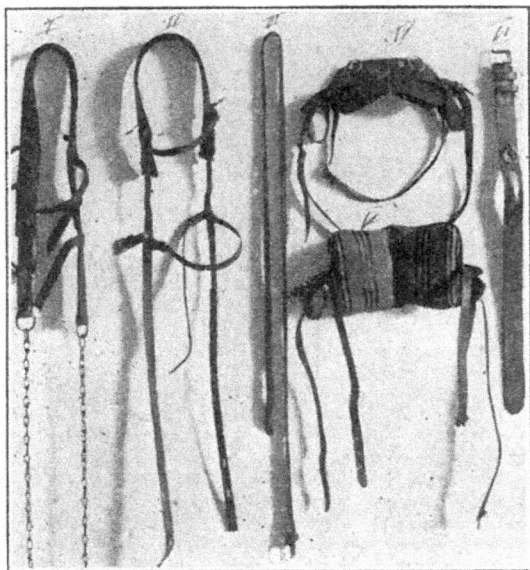

Dog Harness

The regiments to which they were attached had three sections, each of 2 guns and 4 ammunition carts, requiring 36 dogs for the 18 vehicles.

In action the dogs gave every satisfaction, and whilst halted in positions of readiness for often considerable periods, they lay down quietly waiting in their harness.

In coming into action the Nos. 1 had sometimes to creep on in front, accompanied by the team driver of each gun, in order to choose their positions in actions. At a signal, the teams moved quickly up into the emplacements when, the detachments having brought the guns into action, the empty carriages with their drivers proceeded to the rear and rejoined the ammunition carts under cover.

The trials indeed were so successful that orders were issued to erect, for all infantry regiments, kennels for a dozen dogs per unit, and at Beverloo a remount and training establishment for these dogs was to be formed.

It is even reported in the course of the campaign, in Belgium that the war dogs of the machine guns took a still more active part by "going for" German soldiery.

[107]

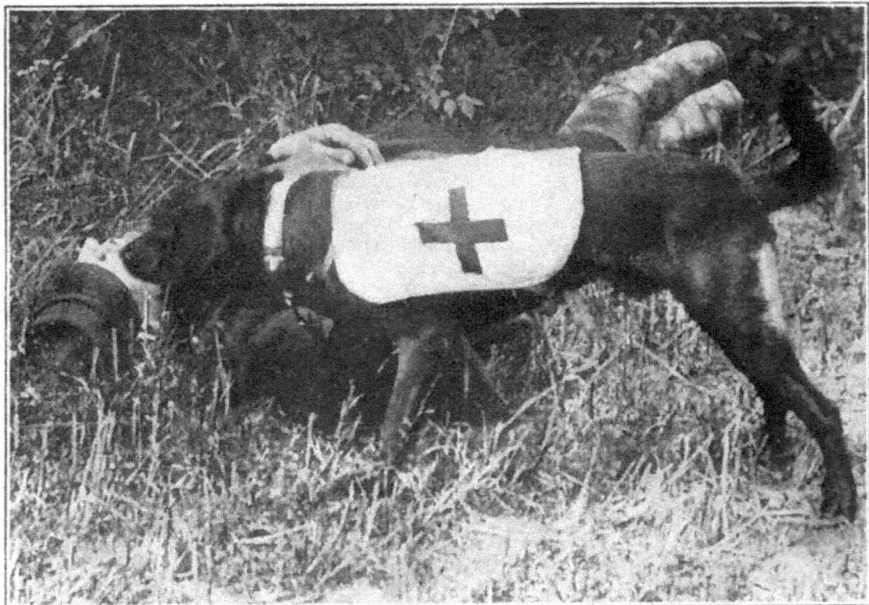

The Ambulance Dog at Work

AMBULANCE DOGS

Not until the history of the present European war comes to be written will it be known just how great have been the services of the dog for ambulance work. Shortly after the outbreak of this, the world's greatest war, an Association in Germany, formed about the year 1893, known as the Ambulance Dogs' Association, greatly increased its activities.

It has been found by experience that the best breeds for ambulance work are collies, retrievers, bloodhounds, Airedale terriers, German shepherd dogs and Dobermann Pinschers. It is absolutely essential that ambulance dogs should be extremely wiry and hardy, and capable of great hardship and endurance, otherwise they are of little use.

The manner in which ambulance dogs are employed is to help the Red Cross men and doctors to search for wounded within a given area on the battlefield. A dog's sense of scent and acute hearing enable him frequently to detect the sound of the breathing of a wounded man when inaudible to the human ear. Moreover, a puff of wind often suffices to carry to the dog's nose the scent of a man lying possibly unconscious in some concealed place.

Fields of battle nowadays are widely extended, and soldiers have to take advantage of every possible bit of natural cover. The instinct of the wounded is to use their last strength in seeking protection from artillery fire, cavalry charges, the wheels of guns, and the other horrors to which they are exposed. They crawl away into the most hidden, safest places. The collection of the wounded is usually at night. This accounts for the large numbers that after each battle are reported as "missing." In some instances the missing have been more than half as many as the known total of killed and wounded.

They are differently equipped in the armies of different countries. The Germans provide their ambulance dogs with a saddle with pockets in which are bandages and dressings, while around the neck is a wooden flask of stimulant. The Italians and French put the flask in a pocket of the saddle. British experts consider bandages and stimulant unnecessary, as every man has to carry his own first-aid dressing, and the extra weight hinders the dog's action. In the English army the dogs wear a very light saddle with the Geneva cross on each side, and a loud bell hangs from a leather collar. The Russians provide their ambulance dogs with small lanterns and attach the bells elsewhere on the collar.

In some of the European armies the ambulance dog is trained to return to his master and guide him to the wounded man; in others he is taught to bark and give the news of his discovery in that way. Still another method is to have the dog on a long leash and thus lead the searcher in the right direction.

The Japanese also use scouting dogs in this way, and so do many of the European armies. They are trained to growl at any sudden surprise, their natural temptation to bark being thwarted by muzzling with a leather strap. In sentry duty the muzzle is moved. With an upwind blowing these sentry dogs are able to detect the approach of men and horses an extraordinary distance away.

On the whole, it is found that the speediest method is for the dog to stay beside his "quarry" when found, and bark until the ambulance arrives, but there is the drawback that if several dogs are being employed in a restricted area and several bark simultaneously, it is not always easy to locate whence the barking comes.

The Germans, unlike the French, do not permit their dogs to wear even a collar, as it is thought that this may hinder him in pushing his way through the thicket or hedges. It has often happened that the wounded are found adjacent to some hedge or other cover not easy to search by human aid alone. On the other hand, the French fasten water bottles around the neck of the dog and train him to search for wounded, who, if still conscious, eagerly grasps the welcome and ofttimes life-saving beverage.

Constant practice in this, as in other kinds of dog training, is an absolute essential. As the war proceeds more and more use will be made of the special functions and gifts of dogs, a resumé of which, when peace again reigns, will surely prove one of the most interesting phases of the hostilities now taking place in Europe.

In the annals of the French army Mustache is still a celebrity. Mustache was one of the war dogs in the Italian campaign when Napoleon was first consul. He saved the French army from a night surprise and annihilation. Later he tracked and captured a spy who had secured valuable information. But this dog's crowning achievement was at the battle of Austerlitz.

The standard bearer of the regiment had just fallen dead. Mustache's teeth and an Austrian soldier's hands grasped the tattered, bloodstained banner simultaneously. Mustache flew at his enemy's throat and bore him down. Then, seizing the flag, he carried it back to the regiment. Napoleon gave Mustache the highest decoration for valor. He met a soldier's death not long afterward, racing forward beside the flag, leading the regiment in a furious charge.

The Canine Ambulance Division of the French Army Off to the Front.

British Sheep Dogs

PUBLIC trials of working sheep dogs were first introduced by Mr. Lloyd Price, of Rhiwlas, Bala, North Wales, in 1873. The object for which they were originally instituted was to promote a better training of sheep dogs amongst the Welsh farmers.

Strange as it may seem, though the mountainous districts of Wales have been devoted from time immemorial almost exclusively to sheep rearing, the old-time farmers took little trouble in the training of dogs to collect and work their sheep. In fact, previous to the inauguration of the competitions, the duties of the Welsh sheep dog were confined principally to the task of hunting and chasing sheep back again up the mountains whenever they strayed down to graze upon the more fertile pastures in the valley which the farmers reserved for their cattle. This was well enough so long as the sheep were roaming at will among their native haunts and feeding grounds, but whenever it was necessary for the farmer to gather his flock together the trouble began. The hardy little animals are wild and timid creatures that are not easily induced to leave their mountain home; moreover, when at liberty they are scattered in small lots over immense tracts of country.

To gather sheep from the mountains with the aid of dogs alone was in those days, with few exceptions, an utter impossibility, consequently as many as ten or twelve men had to be employed to scour the mountains, and even then many stragglers were inevitably left behind. Nowadays all that is changed, one man can with the assistance of a good sheep dog do the same work much more thoroughly and satisfactorily, and without hustling or distressing the sheep themselves.

The systematic training of sheep dogs has indeed accomplished for the sheep-rearing hill farmer almost as much in the way of labor-saving as the adoption of agricultural machinery has done for the farmer who cultivates the lowlands.

The sagacity displayed by a really good sheep-dog gathering sheep upon a mountain side, often a mile or more away from his master, must be seen to be believed. When the farmer goes out to gather his flock for shearing or other purposes, far away upon the bleak hillside, little clusters of white spots are all that are to be seen. The farmer takes up a position upon some point of vantage, gives a word or whistle or instruction to his four-footed companion, and the dog bounds away in response till he seems no more than a tiny moving speck occasionally visible in the distance. Sharp and shrill the farmer's whistle pierces the keen mountain air, and ever and anon, as though by magic, the little white dots begin to move and converge towards a common center. In response to one signal the sound of the dog's answering bark can be heard; another signal and he drops as though shot, and is as silent as the grave. In the dim distance a few small dots can be seen; they are some stragglers that have been overlooked; a whistle galvanizes them also into motion, but in the wrong direction; a moment later and they are merged into one motionless white blot upon the dark mountain side. The blot moves again, not quite in the desired direction; whistle succeeds whistle in quick succession, and at each one the little moving blot alters its course, zig-zagging this way and that, until it finally becomes merged in the large white patch that marks the remainder of the flock, which keeps on the move, drawing nearer and nearer until the sheep take shape and can be seen coming down steadily with the dog dodging in their rear, till they are rounded up and brought to a standstill within reach of the farmer's stick. Such a sight is common today upon the Welsh mountain or in the Scottish Highlands, though it is not given to every man to acquire perfect mastery over his animal; so much depends upon both man and dog. A dog belonging to a man who takes no interest, or has not the knack and patience necessary to teach him is worse than useless. The dog often reflects to a great extent his master's character. An excitable, hasty-tempered man generally has a headstrong, willful dog that is hard to control. Some dogs, born of a long line of carefully-trained sheep dogs, take to working sheep as ducks do to water; a savage, uncontrollable brute, whose only ambition seems to be to worry and abuse the sheep, and there are hundreds of such animals, is simply a hindrance and a source of trouble to its owner, as anyone who is acquainted with sheep and their ways knows full well.

The sheep dog proper must above all things be gentle and patient with its often cantankerous charges, yet firm and masterful enough to inspire the timid sheep with sufficient sense of fear to cause them to move away in another direction at its appearance and approach without creating such a panic-stricken stampede. Such strains of dogs are scarce and highly-prized by their owners, though from the show-bench fancier's point of view their often nondescript exterior cannot be classified into those niceties of shape and color in which the judge of show dogs delight. Many a sheep dog that would not attract a second glance from a professional dog judge has won enough in money prizes to turn the whole fraternity green with envy.

Such a dog is, for instance, Mr. J. Moses' "Old Jem," not beautiful to look at, but of sterling quality, which has won for his master over $1,000 in cash quite irrespective of the value of himself and his progeny.

Sheep-dog trials are now held in all parts of the British Empire, Canada, New Zealand, Australia; in fact, wherever sheep are reared in any quantity.

Perhaps one of the most favorable opportunities the general public has of watching one of these absorbingly interesting spectacles is during the well-known agricultural show held each year in Lord Rothchild's beautiful park at Tring, England. A description of an actual trial witnessed by the writer in these ideal surroundings will give an idea of the exciting nature of the tests and high standard of perfection to which the numerous entries have to be trained before they can compete with the remotest chance of success.

A portion of the vast park, some three-quarters of a mile long and about half as wide, remote from the show ground where the exhibits are localized, is divided off by a rope fence; this constitutes the course, of which thousands can obtain a full and uninterrupted view. The competitor takes up his stand near the center with his dog or dogs, for there are prizes for two dogs working together as well as for single dog

When "Penning," the Man Is Allowed to Assist the Dog.

trials. The number of sheep that have to be driven round the course is three only; this small number greatly increases the difficulties of the subsequent maneuvers. Fresh sheep are provided for each competitor, usually those of the wild, hardy mountain variety.

At a given signal the animals are released from a cart that is out of sight in a clump of trees on a hill some half a mile distant. The dog must then locate the sheep, the master remaining in the center of the course guiding and directing him by voice or whistle as he chooses. The obstacles consist of, first, what is termed "a false fence"; that is to say, two short lines of hurdles so placed as to leave a wide gap through which the dog must drive the sheep; should he allow them to run round the end of one of the lines instead of through the center, the sheep must be driven back and another attempt made. The second obstacle is a flag-post, round which the sheep must be driven in a circle before being conducted through a V-shaped gap made with two hurdles.

If the dog has negotiated these obstacles successfully he will have brought his charges to within about a hundred yards of his master. Having been successful in bringing the sheep so far, a very different task awaits both dog and master at the

[111]

"Maltese Cross." At this, and the final "penning up" of the sheep, the master is permitted by the rules of the trials, to assist his dog personally. The "Maltese Cross" consists of two lanes intersecting at right angles, each passage being only just sufficiently wide to permit the sheep to pass in single file. It must not be imagined that the wild mountain sheep, terrified at their unwonted surroundings and the presence of a strange dog, submit tamely to being thus driven past alternative openings without strenuous efforts to break away and bolt in whichever direction their erratic fancy dictates. The master must be on the alert for these attempts, and be quick and decisive in giving his dog instruction as to how to frustrate these sudden rushes. It is upon the promptitude and correctness with which the dog responds to the signals that success or failure depends. It is at the cross that the innate perversity of the sheep's nature asserts itself, with the result that the first animal very frequently turns down one or other of the cross lanes instead of going straight through. When this occurs the other two naturally follow, and all three must be induced to negotiate the passage again. Having driven the sheep through straight in one direction, the dog and his master must then bring them back and run them through the other lane at right angles to the original course. Finally, the even more difficult task of "penning up" awaits the competitors. The final pen is formed of four hurdles with a space just sufficient to admit one sheep at a time left open. The slightest over-anxiety on the part of the dog or his master is fatal at this stage of the trial. The difficulty of exercising the necessary self-restraint will be the more readily realized when one

The Sheep Being Driven Through the Maltese Cross.

considers that it is often a matter of working against time, as should a dog have been a little slow or unfortunate in his previous maneuvers he is extremely liable to exceed the time limit set for the competition, and thus lose the points awarded for penning.

It cannot be laid down as an infallible rule that the best dog for actual field work will always win a competition, so much relies on the master and other incidental details which affect the judge's decision.

The most important consideration from the competitor's point of view is the invididuality of the three sheep which the dog is called upon to work. Some, when released, are found to be extremely wild, and cause the dog a lot of trouble by frantic efforts to escape. Others often adopt an aggressive attitude towards the dog, and persist in facing round and charging at him instead of allowing themselves to be driven. This type of sheep is most exasperating, both to dog and man. Again, many dogs, more especially young ones, are excitable by the applause of the spectators.

To see sheep dogs work to perfection one should watch them, as the writer has been privileged to do, being practiced and trained upon their own home ground, where one can realize more fully the practical utility of a well-trained dog and the amount of labor which he saves his owner. The north of England and some parts of Scotland have always been noted for good dogs, the original strain being a cross between the smooth collie and the old Scotch bearded collie. These animals are naturally hardy, fleet-footed and sagacious, and for real skill in working sheep will hold their own against any dogs in the world.

One of the most prominent and successful trainers is Mr. J. Moses, of Oswestry, who is manager of Lord Harlech's Home Farm at Brogyntyn, and the accompanying photographs show some of his famous dogs at work on the farm. Mr. Moses is a great advocate of teaching a dog to work entirely by whistle, instead of giving commands in ordinary language. The great advantage of this system is that the dog can hear and recognize the signals at a much greater distance, and when once accustomed to them is much less liable to misinterpret his master's meaning than is the case when the command is given vocally. Many people seem to find a difficulty in training their dogs to work by whistle, but if the system is started at the commencement of a young dog's training he will soon learn to appreciate the distinctions of sounds and obey them more readily.

In order to demonstrate the perfect command that my friend had over the actions of his dog, even at a great distance, for it must have been over three-quarters of a mile, Mr. Moses made "Trim" execute a series of maneuvers, instructing the dog to drive the sheep round a telegraph post, in and out of two trees, take them back again to the original spot in which they were first located, and finally drive them straight up to within reach of his master's stick. Each and every one of these evolutions was carried out with such skill, intelligence and obedience on the part of the dog that it seemed hard at first to realize that "Trim" was actually obeying implicitly his master's command, and not just driving the sheep about for his own pleasure.

The maneuvering of sheep at a distance is a feature in sheep-dog trials for which more points than are now granted should be given, as it demonstrates unmistakably the excellence of the training and also the actual utility of a dog for field work. Many dogs are under perfect control as long as they are within reach of their master's stick, but cannot be relied upon implicitly when far away; such a dog is obviously improperly trained.

Patience and firmness are the keynotes of success in training a sheep dog, though everything relies, in the first instance, upon the suitability of the dog taken in hand, for good sheep dogs are born as well as made, and a well-bred puppy will have a natural instinct for the work, which will reveal itself at an early age.

In the next chapter will be found some useful hints on the training of the working sheep dog.

Training the Working Shepherd Dog

C ERTAIN technical terms are used in the following article which it may be well to explain for the benefit of those not familiar with the shepherd's vocabulary.

1. The "run out" means that the dog is sent away to gather the sheep. "Running out" is the act of going for the sheep.

2. "Hauling" in its widest sense means the dog going out for his sheep, taking command of them and bringing them to the shepherd. In the narrower sense, however, the term is confined to the bringing in of the sheep by the dog.

3. "Shedding" means the dividing of a lot of sheep. Supposing, for example, a shepherd wishes to separate lambs from their mothers, the act of doing so by the dog is called "shedding."

4. "Wearing" means keeping a sheep from going in the wrong direction. Supposing, for example, a sheep bolts up a wrong road, the dog is sent to turn it back. Turning back is the "wearing."

5. A "cut" simply refers to a number of sheep. Supposing, for example, a shepherd herds five or six hundred sheep and goes for forty or fifty to take them to the market. The number so taken is called a "cut."

6. "Flying off" means where the dog yields to the sheep instead of facing up to them. In "wearing" this is best seen. A dog which will not come in close to stubborn sheep, yields to them when pressed, is said to "fly off."

7. A "soft-tempered" dog is one which shows little grit when pressed by wild or stubborn sheep. It won't stand up to them and shows little fight, and generally evidence of a soft disposition. The contrary expression is "hard tempered," which means a dog that will not yield to wild or stubborn sheep, but will face up to them, and as a last resort will even grip and show his teeth and other signs of temper and determination.

Believing that some instruction as to the methods employed in the training of the working collie will be helpful to those who desire to bring out the best gifts with which Nature has endowed this king of all utility dogs, we append a few suggestions from the curriculum of Mr. T. P. Brown, of Oxton, Berwickshire, Scotland, than whom no one is more qualified to speak on this important subject.

In the first place, it must be acknowledged that unless the master has himself studied the subject with the utmost care and keen perception, success in teaching a dog to work sheep will not fall to his lot. Many a good dog has been spoiled in the hands of an unthinking and unsympathetic would-be trainer, and, conversely, many a vicious, timid, or "wild" dog has been converted by the master hand into a brainy, intelligent servant.

With few exceptions, any collie can be taught to work sheep; therefore, as a general proposition, it is the man who makes or mars the dog's natural bent.

To achieve the greatest measure of success the sooner one starts the elementary first lessons the better. The puppy should be taken in hand when three or four months old.

The very first step is to teach him to run up to you. Use a thin, low whistle with the lips, and pat and make a fuss of him when he comes up.

The second lesson is to get him to go down quickly. This is best done by a hiss. If he does not put his head down, press it gently down with your hand. This has generally to be repeated a good many times before he does it nicely. Some pups go down of their own accord when they see the sheep. This is no real drawback, but as a rule they require a little more training to go down *when commanded*, instead of waiting till they get to a place where they want to go down.

After the pup has learned to go down nicely, put him down and walk away, and see if he will lie still until you give him the whistle to come up, and don't rest satisfied until he does so with alacrity.

When he has learned to do this to please you, begin to stop him half-way up, and always see that he puts his head in the proper position. He should be proficient in this before he is ever taken to the sheep. No pup should ever be taken to the sheep until he is under complete control in the run up and lay down. To introduce him to sheep until he has thoroughly mastered these simple but highly-important commands has a tendency to spoil him and get him into bad habits. No matter how fast he is running, if you give him the hiss to stop he should drop like a stone; and, on the other hand, he should obey the command to come on quickly and without the least hesitation, and on no account should he rise until told to do so. To fall and rise when commanded, and *only* when commanded, is the most important point in the training of a collie. Having progressed so far, the pup should now be taken to the sheep.

If he is off a good working strain, he will either circle away round his "quarry" or he will "set" and crawl forward.

If he circles round and goes down, and the sheep do not come away, he is apt to lie still, but if you use the call whistle and bring him a little forward, then drop him. The sheep will most likely come away, and you must take care that he comes straight behind them, and not too quickly.

Don't use the call whistle very long at first, just a little to get him to understand to start the sheep. Get him used to start either with a sheep or a short whistle.

If in running up to the sheep he does not go right round, you must go up to the sheep and move them in the direction you want them to go. Then use the whistle, sound or words by which you want to shift him (some trainers say "Keep wide" or "Keep wide, away out," but it is better to use only distinctive whistles).

You should thus keep the sheep moving about, making him move to what spot you want. Others use a combination of whistles and signs (motions of the arms). This latter method has its advantages when working at a distance and under certain climatic conditions.

When the dog has become expert in moving about, teach him to "run out." Don't try him too far away at first, and if possible let him see the sheep.

A perfect run out should be in the form of a good wide circle all the way until he gets well behind the sheep. Then he should double back behind the sheep when he sees he has them all rounded up, and he should be allowed to move them a little before you put him down.

In "haulding" them he should come straight behind the sheep, and not too near them. If they come steadily, he should be allowed to follow them in. When "haulding" a few sheep, say five, he should bring them in straight; but with a large number he should "flank" them from side to side in half-moon circles, as by this means he gets them forward in better time.

By this time the dog should have learned to go down at a distance from the shepherd, a distance which is only restricted by the impossibility of hearing the whistle,

[114]

In all these processes one requires four different kinds of whistles—one for the "call," one to go out, one to stop and lie down, and one to hauld.

To teach a dog "to shed," get the sheep to pass quietly between yourself and the dog several times; the dog during this time must lie down.

Then divide the sheep and give him the call whistle to come in to you, and drop him when he is in between the two lots. Then go behind one of the lots and press them on to the dog and get him "to wear" and turn them to you.

Repeat this several times, and in giving the call whistle make sure that he never rises until commanded, for a dog that moves about as the sheep move will never be a good "shedder," as he always mixes the sheep up when you are preparing for a "cut." Be sure also that he shifts every time you ask him, and that he turns the sheep in to you, instead of flying off them.

At this stage in his education the dog should be approaching his complete training. To teach him to come in front of the sheep, draw him to you by the call whistle. He will think at first that he is to come in to you, but when you see he is far enough past the sheep to give him plenty of room to work, give him the whistle to go to the sheep. He will then turn and face the sheep, and as he does so drop him there. After being several times repeated he will do this as readily as he has learned to go round behind the sheep.

The next lesson is to teach him to go from one side to the other, passing between you and the sheep.

Let him go half round the sheep, then get him to go forward on the sheep from any point he is stopped, by either driving straight from you or from the left side to the right side. This feat is most necessary for driving away or for pole work at a trial.

The art of wearing a single sheep has not been touched on, because unless the dog is naturally gifted with this it is almost impossible to make him proficient at it, though one can help him a little.

Much depends on the nerve and compelling power of the dog's eye. Leave him pretty well to his own resources until he has the sheep stopped before you drop him.

Some pups are naturally born with tendencies to wearing single sheep, including to run too wide or too near, and, worst of all, stopping before they go round the sheep. Be guarded to immediately check these faults, and remember that command is the most important lesson of all.

One hears a great deal about bad-tempered dogs and soft-tempered ones, but it is not so much a display of temper as nervousness. If a dog keeps his eye on the sheep, no matter how soft he is in the temper, any capable trainer can make him a good dog, but the one who won't keep his eye on the sheep can never become proficient in his service to his lord and master.

Police Dogs

IT is admitted on all hands that the dog is capable of training to do his master's bidding in a great many different ways.

Other chapters appear in this work detailing with what purpose he is used as an aid to the hunter, sportsman, courser, for the drawing of quick-firing guns into the firing line, for ambulance work, for sentry duty, as an indispensable aid in all Arctic and Antarctic expeditions, to say nothing of the sport certain breeds give us as racing and performing dogs.

The purport of this chapter is to indicate with what success he is being trained as a branch of the police force. Thousands of dogs, mostly of the German and Belgian sheepdog variety, are at this present time enrolled in the widely scattered police and other municipal forces of America and other countries.

In the training of dogs for this work a special aptitude on the part of the "handler" or "guide" is essential. Given a reasonable amount of common sense, unlimited patience and an understanding of a dog's nature, success is assured in a large majority of cases.

The police dog trial is an old story so far as Germany, Belgium and Holland are concerned. Americans are now taking this highly instructive work in hand and the displays create a tremendous amount of enthusiastic interest. The objects of such trials are:
1. Obedience exercises.
2. Detective work.
3. Protective work.
The obedience exercises called for are:
1. Heeling on leash.
2. Heeling without leash. The guide turns to right or left. Runs, walks and stops with the object of confusing the dog.

The Police Dog is Trained to Attack on Command

3. Refusing food offered by strangers or thrown or found on the ground. The dog is made to lie down both free and in the absence of the guide, and he must refuse bread, meat or other tempting morsels of food. Then a dish of food is placed within his reach, but he must not touch it under penalty of lost points.

4. Guarding objects. This is considered a most important acquisition. Every possible effort is made to remove the object by the judge. The dog is chained beside the object, which is well within his reach, and he is taught to lie to lie down quietly beside it and not to move or growl or show his teeth until the judge makes an effort to take the object away quietly. If a vigorous attempt is made to snatch the object then the dog is to defend it and himself in energetic fashion. Even when the judge threatens the dog with a stick, or by coaxing, the faithful tyke will be proof against them all. Bad marks are recorded if he gnaws the object or otherwise misuses it.

5. Giving "tongue" on command. This must be done continuously on command. It is insufficient for him to bark once and imitation barking by the guide is forbidden.

6. Retrieving objects weighing two pounds. The dog must sit down quietly and await instructions. Then he must bring it coming over a fence or hedge promptly and sit down again before his guide until relieved of the object. The varying heights of the fence or wall provide a number of diverse exercises in the retrieving lesson.

9. Scaling wall.

10. Going ahead. The guide walks across the trial ground with the dog at heel On command the dog runs ahead in the direction given to a distance of about 30 yards. He shall "drop" immediately on command and stay there until told to rise.

11. Lying down. The dog is shown free in this exercise and immediately on command he must rise and go away.

The detective work is conducted as follows:

1. Searching for objects left by a stranger at the end of a trail of 250 yards long and half an hour old. The trailer proceeds on a track, directed by the judge, walk at his natural pace and at the end of the trail stand still for one minute, wipe his feet well on the ground, place the object between his footprints and then take the shortest cut to a place again directed by the judge. An interesting variation of this is provided by the object being placed thirty yards away from the end of trail and at right angles thereto.

[116]

Police Dog Scaling Fence 8 ft. 6 in. High

2. Search for object left by a stranger on a trail 500 yards long, and barking at the trailer when found. This is done both with the dog free and also when on leash ten yards long, and it is particularly desirable that the dog be taught to bark on finding the object or person discovered.

The protective work comprises:

1. Scouting over ground and barking at any large object found. The dog follows the direction indicated by the guide and covers the ground carefully, searching every nook and corner not so as to encircle the guide at a short distance. Three hiding places are provided. As soon as the dog finds the hidden person he is taught to watch him and by barking attract the guide's attention.

2. Transporting "prisoner" without nipping. When found, the dog follows behind the "prisoner" quietly without barking or nipping. Any object dropped inconspicuously must be picked up at once by the dog and brought to the guide, then continue the transport without waiting for the command. If the "prisoner" attempts to escape, or attacks the guide, the dog must attack him immediately, without waiting for command to do so. During these attacks the "prisoner" shoots twice into the air.

3. Watching the "prisoner" quietly when latter is quiet.

4. Arresting and holding the "prisoner" on attempted flight. The "prisoner" attempts to drive the dog away with blows or a whip or by throwing pieces of wood at him. The dog must watch him alone and twice stop an attempted flight. As soon as the "prisoner" is quiet the dog must leave him alone and watch him until the guide returns.

A high percentage of points are given for general obedience.

The whole attitude of the dog is taken into consideration especially between the different exercises if he remains at heel; also how he controls himself between the exercises toward the "prisoner," and whether he needs holding in check by the collar and in other ways indicates that he understands when he is on duty and when he is not.

Unquestionably these trials throw a good deal of light on the training of dogs used by the Continental nations for war purposes as well as for police work, and it is hoped that greater facilities will be given for such in other parts of the world.

The Hunting World and the Use of Dogs

IT IS to the Normans that the English-speaking races of the earth today owe their hunting hounds and in all their varieties. The Talbot hound was introduced into England at the time of the conquest by William the First.

All are not agreed as to the color of these Talbot hounds. Somervile, the great sporting poet, describes them as "white as Alpine snows." There is, however, reason to believe that they are invariably of a reddish tan and often with a black saddle. In form, color and shape they are very much like the English bloodhound of today; indeed, that noble animal is supposed to be the bedrock of all the breeds of hunting hounds that are now in use the world over; and this because of that sentiment and recognition of the variety as the chief pillar or the stay of several of the most valued breeds, that the bloodhound is placed first in the stud books of England and America, and the breed is number one in the catalogues of the all-round dog shows everywhere.

English Foxhounds in Full Cry

It was and is desirable that the head of a hunting hound should be of the above description—that is, if a close-hunting, unerring hound is required to hunt singly, rather than in a pack. The formation of the head above described, is one that is "made" for the purposes of hunting; and in such a head are to be found the highly developed olfactory nerves which communicate with the brain and actually inform the hound when he strikes the scent of an animal and whether the effluvium is recent or old.

It is the gloriousness and health-giving surroundings that have made the chase so popular with nearly all peoples, and that is the reason hounds are bred with such care and may generally be found in the ownership of the well-to-do and the high personages of the world.

In the early days the English pursued the chase on foot, and their objects of pursuit appear to have been principally the wild boar and the wolf. The Anglo-Normans might be considered as the more polished, more noble, and more scientific hunters, and they introduced that powerful and pleasant assistant in the chase—the horse—as well as a great variety of objects of pursuit. They chased the stag, the roebuck, the fox, the hare, etc., and hunting the less dangerous animals seems to have constituted their principal amusements; though the wolf and the boar occasionally occupied their attention, and in all these branches of the hunt dogs of varying degree were used.

[118]

Every village in England has its beagles, and nothing is more enjoyable than an old-fashioned fox hunting, or chase, where hounds belonging to many owners are packed together, and, jumping a fox, they run him for hours on end, their glorious music resounding throughout the woods and delighting the ear of the sportsman. The American foxhound appears to have more of the old harrier or English southern hound blood in him than is allowed to remain in the hound of the English. There are some broad-headed and long-eared and heavy-lipped hounds in the United States which remind the observer of the hounds of France and other Continental countries—hounds that still bear a good deal of resemblance to the old talbot-hounds—the hounds of the Normans. Finer and finer the English bred their hounds as stag hunting gave way to fox hunting. The old staghound was only one remove from the talbot, and he was a big and picturesque creature and these hounds are to be found in France today.

Hunting is a foremost sport all over the world, and there can be little wonder that the spirit and standing of the peoples may be gauged from the quality of their hounds The panoply of the chase is among the more glorious sights of the world, and in the pursuance of the various sports connected with hounds, large and small, a vast amount of money is spent, and a large number of persons employed, in the piping times of peace.

The beagle should be 15 inches or under, measured across the withers. If he is over that height he becomes a harrier;; and a harrier over 19 inches becomes a fox-hound, and a foxhound standing 24 inches at the shoulders and 30 inches round his girth is indeed a splendid creature and a beautifully proportioned one to boot. The hound is indeed a beauty and a joy forever!

In England alone there are more than 800 packs of hunting dogs. Roughly, there are 326 owners of hunts or hunting establishments in France. Some of these hunts have 50 or 60 couples. In Belgium foxhounds are kept, and the chief packs of hounds in Germany are the Royal Hounds, at Potsdam, and the Hanover Hounds. They both hunt the drag and the boar. The conditions of hunting in Austria and Hungary are much better than in Germany. It is a good wild country and full of foxes. The Roman hounds are world renowned. Fox hunting was introduced into Italy by Lord Chesterfield in 1842, and the sport has flourished ever since. In Spain the Calpa fox-hounds show much sport in the vicinity of Gibraltar.

· In the United States there are about forty well-known and properly established packs of foxhounds. Throughout the Indian Empire there are numerous packs, many of them being of the bobbery or mixed kind. The jackal is the most frequently hunted animal. The Bombay Hounds are the chief pack in India.

In South Africa the jackal is hunted with foxhounds, and a single hound is used to drive buck to the rifle or gun. American foxhounds have recently been introduced to British East Africa for the purposes of hunting lion. These hounds have been of great use in bagging such large and dangerous game, and in the case of cheetah and other tree-climbing animals, the American foxhounds have not had the slightest difficulty in driving their quarry at such a pace and with so much persistence that the large cat is glad to see the supposed shelter of a thorn or other tree standing out like a sentinel on the vast expanse of plains.

The foxhound, the harrier and the beagle are also of great use in Africa for driving certain of the antelope, which keep in the bush, to the gun, and a good deal of sport may be had in some of the rivers otter hunting, and when otter hunting, a monitor, or huge lizard-like creature, is often started in a swamp, and the reptile, taking to the water like an otter, he will provide a good deal of sport. The otters in the Eastern province of South Africa are plentiful and of good size. The rivers are very huntable, for they are not deep and there is no great width or volume of water at certain seasons of the year. There is much sport to be had on the Mooi River, in Natal, where a pack of pure-bred otter hounds is kept. And these hounds will not only hunt the water dog but the aforesaid African monitor. Everywhere the hound is useful and especially is this the case in a big and open country like Africa, where a dog is required to be not only a hunter, but a guard and a friend.

In Australia there is a good deal of hunting and the Melbourne hunt is a well-organized institution. Australia is a country in which all animal life increases and multiplies rapidly. In 1864 one dog fox and two vixens were imported from England. There soon became enough foxes in Victoria to last the colony, now the province, forever. But red deer and kangaroos are sometimes hunted with foxhounds, and in Western Australia, in the neighborhoods of Freemantle, Perth and Kalgoorlie, there has been much sport experienced in hunting the brush-tailed kangaroos. This form of hunting was introduced by Mr. Cairns Candy in the late nineties.

In Tasmania, the island province off the main Australian continent, there is some hunting with properly constituted and maintained packs of hounds. In this lovely country, noted for its apples and the matchless complexions of its pretty women, they hunt deer and hare. In New Zealand there is a good deal of hunting, and harriers are principally in use. There is a fine open country, and that in the North Island will remind the hunting man of some of the shires of England.

The hounds of Europe, Asia, Africa and Australasia have been discussed, and now we will find ourselves back in America. And this country may well be proud of its old-fashioned, long-eared, heavy-jawed and deep-throated foxhounds. That American foxhounds are suitable for hunting American foxes, and where foxes are shot before hounds, there can be no manner of doubt; but they do not kill many foxes, neither may this killing quality be placed to the credit of the English foxhounds in this country. Once a fox is able to sit down and listen to his pursuers, then a foxhound or a pack of foxhounds, have as much chance of overtaking the quarry as a short-winged hawk has of catching a swallow on the wing. A century ago, it is recorded, it was not unusual in South Carolina to drive out of one large swamp, deer, wolves, bears, foxes, wildcats and wild turkeys. The sportsmen were ready to shoot all of these.

In descriptive poetry of the earliest date, hunting is frequently alluded to; even in the most important action of the whole Iliad, the death of Hector, the pursuit of him by Achilles is thus introduced:

"As through the forest, o'er the vale and lawn,
The well-breathed beagle drives the flying fawn,
In vain he tries the coverts of the brakes,
Or deep beneath the trembling thicket shakes,
Sure of the vapor in the tainted dews,
The certain hound his various maze pursues."

—*Pope.*

The Gun and Coursing Dogs of the World

IF there be one study in connection with dogs more interesting than another, it must be that which has reference to the gun dogs and the coursing dogs of the world. Since time immemorial, dogs have been used by man for certain purposes and those which he has bred, maintained and improved for his services, have kept time with the ever-changing methods whereby the human is able to obtain and have for himself the beasts of the field and the birds of the air. The first men who went after game hunted it for food; and they very soon found out the most suitable dogs for their purposes and they bred and produced dogs for different kinds of work. It is fair to write that no domestic animals are better represented throughout the world than are thoroughbred dogs of one kind or another. The pure-breeds are to be found in countries that are foreign to their varieties, and what is more, they are highly and justly prized by their owners and even the very community in which the imported dog has its new being. For let it be known, there are less distinctions than owning a superior dog, and as these dogs are capable of reproducing themselves, and both the males and females are prolific breeders, there is almost at once, or within one year, established in the kennel of the new land the high-blooded and moreover most useful dogs of other nations. And that is the reason that wherever we may go we shall probably find the particularly good gun dogs of Great Britain. These consist of the pointer, the English, Irish and Gordon setters, the retrievers and the Labrador or Lesser Newfoundland dogs, and the various spaniels, which have all been practically made perfect in the British Isles and distributed to the four corners of the earth. Dogs have been produced that will hunt as well in one country as another; but one can generally find that dogs—gun dogs and coursing dogs—are mostly chosen with an eye to the environment in which they will have to hunt.

Both the pointer and the spaniel originally came from Spain, so it is said. But the original Spanish pointer was too heavy and slow in his pace for the English gunner, so he was crossed with the lighter foxhound, and it is even said with the greyhound, so that he should be more active and able to cover his ground better. Furthermore, the heavy-headed Spanish pointer had the kind of head and lips that proclaim a hunting dog that is inclined to keep his nose to the ground, rather than carry it highly and thus better obtain the body scent of birds and other game in the distance. The setter was originally the large spaniel, and was taught to "set" or sit down when he had come upon birds, so that the game could be encompassed by the fall-net, or the hawk or

A Fine Group of Gun Dogs.

falcon might have the better opportunity to fly at her quarry. When the small pellets of lead were invented and the shotgun first used then the setters of the netters and falconers became gun dogs, and as such we will find pointers, setters, retrievers and spaniels of English origin in every country where the sportsman may be found. Gun and coursing dogs are not only imported into America as workers but as show dogs, and in the great majority of cases these dogs are thoroughly broken or trained as well as being good to look upon. Then these gun dogs may compete at the various field trials now run off all over Europe, the United States and Canada, or even South Africa, or at the coursing meetings in every country of the world. The coursing dog is found

The Hunter and His Dog

most useful in Canada, especially in the prairie provinces, where coyotes are destructive and a curse to the sheepman and even the horse breeder, for a pack of prairie wolves will attack and kill a foal. As a part and parcel of the farm, the ranch, the station and estancia the gun dog and the coursing dogs are invaluable. Pointers, setters, spaniels and retrievers are useful under all circumstances, and they perform the same work in all climates and under the various and dissimilar conditions. In some countries pointers are preferred to setters; but, on inquiry, it will generally be found that the alleged fitness of one variety of dog over the other, is merely a matter of taste or "fancy." A man who owns setters prefers setters; the individual who possesses pointers has a preference for pointers. 'Tis his fancy—his hobby, and that gentle leaning towards one breed often means the fellow's antipathy to another breed.

In a land or country that has been indifferently cultivated or is wild, there are several kinds of burrs that inconveniently fall at the very time when the hunting or shooting season begins. Some say that the pointer, because of his short coat, will not be so troubled with these prickles as will the long-coated setter, which is feathered on the legs and picks up the burrs wherever he may go. On the other hand, the setter admirer avows that the feathered and better protected foot of the setter saves him from being lamed so often as the clean and unprotected footed pointer. So it will be seen that these preferences are mostly imaginary and may be traced to fancy.

On the Continent of Europe we find many kinds of most useful dogs; but both the pointers and setters are only modifications of the old hunting dogs that came from Spain. There are rough-haired and smooth-coated pointers in Germany, and they are very handsome animals with excellent formation and with hunting qualities of the highest order. The griffons of France, Holland and Belgium are particularly good dogs; rough and ready in appearance, with excellent brains and great scenting powers. In him we will recognize a lot of hound blood which may have come from the otter-hound or the hounds of Vendee. But they are just the sort of dogs that a man wants for rough-shooting in the woods or swamps. The griffon is an active dog, does not throw his tongue when immediately close to game or in sight of it, as does the hound. The griffon makes a good woodcock, "partridge" and duck dog; and as such he has been found of the greatest use in America. The griffon is a good dog in the water as well as on land, and in this way he proves himself a thoroughly serviceable all-round sporting dog. The wolf-hounds of Russia are most useful dogs, and as their name foretells, they are used as wolf-coursing dogs. Three are slipped to the wolf after he has been driven from cover by foxhounds or beaters. When they come up with their game they bump into the quarry and at the right moment lay hold of the beast by the neck and hold him until the hunter arrives and either dispatches the game with a pistol or knife, or placing a stick in the wolf's jaws, twists a rope around the muzzle and neck, and thus preventing him from accomplishing any harm, captures the creature alive and practically uninjured. The Russian wolf-hound is the best killer of any of the coursing dogs. Like a bulldog, he holds on to what he seizes; his jaws are very powerful, and it is because of this tenacity that the Russian wolf-hound, or borzoi, as he is frequently called, is used for crossing purposes on the English greyhound and the Scottish deerhound or on the progeny of these two breeds, for the purpose of producing what is known as the "long dog" of the Canadian prairies, where he is used principally for coursing and killing the coyote. The Russian wolf-hound has also been successfully crossed on to the deerhound in Australia, either for straight out kangaroo dogs or dingo killers. The Russian wolf-hound goes to the throat of his enemy, and such a dog is required for the prompt killing of dingoes. The long and strong limbs of the kangaroo are means of defense, both as propelling powers in his long and swift bounds or jumps and for fighting when it comes to the more serious defense as against dingoes or the domesticated dogs, hence the kangaroo dog is taught to attack from behind.

The slugi or greyhounds of Arabia, Persia and Egypt may be noticed. In these we will find small examples of the Russian wolf-hound, but they have down or setter-like ears as opposed to the half-cocked or fully pricked ears of the Northern dogs. The dogs of the near East have generally long feet and these are feathered, as are their ears, legs and tails. They are used to course antelopes and hares, and one of the most ancient of sports is to not only course the antelope with these slugi, but at the same time fly hawks at the fleeing buck, which has the advantage over the dogs in sandy places and over stony or rocky ground. The big and somewhat picturesque greyhounds of Afghanistan are large dogs much after the form of the near Eastern dogs; they are used for the same purposes, and because of their surroundings in high altitudes, they grow large and wooly coats to aid them against the vicissitudes of the cold climate. In India, indeed, all over Asia, the different gun dogs generally associated with the British Isles are used and they cannot very well be done without on the small feathered game which is plentiful. In Japan and China the pheasant shooting is very good, and Americans who have gone over to shoot in those countries have taken their dogs from this country with them and have found them to accomplish all that was required of them.

If we leave Asia and continue our wanderings and huntings to the South, and reach Africa, we will find plenty of work for our hunting hounds, our coursing dogs and gun dogs. The slugi or greyhounds were the most valued dogs of the Pharoahs. In the ancient monuments the dogs' places are at the sides of some great personage. It would appear that the tastes of the Egyptians of old were exactly those of the ancient Britons, for there is an old Welsh saying which states that "a gentleman is known by his horse, his hawk and his greyhound." The slugi in its native or home state is now principally to be found in its purity among the Bedouin Arabs. They place the greatest value on these dogs, and they are as difficult to obtain from the wandering Arabs as are their thoroughbred horses. Furthermore, there is an Arab saying that the most valued of all things among the highest of these nomads and hunters are "his horse, his slugi and his wife's earrings." The Arabian greyhounds are primarily valuable for coursing antelope in sandy countries and where the sun is felt with all his power. They also thrive in temperate climates.

Our old friends the pointers and setters are used in Northern Africa, as they are in the South and the East, the West and Central of that enormous and game-holding country. American foxhounds have been found most useful running on the trail of the lion; furthermore, they have the good sense to keep away from the great cat when it comes to close quarters. These hounds will soon tree a cheetah and the rifles or the arrows of the natives will accomplish the rest. In Africa, generally, there is much bird life, as that term applies to partridges, snipe, quail, etc. In that country there are several small and dangerous snakes; but it has been found that the dogs'

Incident in a Waterloo Coursing Meeting

sagacity has been such that they, of their own initiation, immediately become alive to the dangerous natures of these reptiles and that they will return to the shooter when they get near a snake, either in the grass or on a branch overhead. Greyhounds are used in Africa for coursing the smaller bucks and hares, and such dogs, fleet of foot and able to run down an antelope, may be bartered "up-country" for produce of great value, the natives, especially the chiefs of powerful tribes —practically nations—having been known to give mining and other concessions where first class dogs have been given as presents.

There is a great deal of variety in the Australian shooting and the bush life of that lovely country is entrancing for the lover of nature and the observer of mammals and birds. Pointers and setters are used in just the same way as they are anywhere else. Quail are plentiful and the varieties of numbers of wild fowl are beautiful and often countless. As for hares, in some places they are almost as common as the rabbits; and hares are three times more prolific in that balmy country than they are in climes north of the equator in Europe and America. Coursing is a great sport there and is a means of much speculating or wagering among Australians and New Zealanders. New Zealand in many climatic instances and country surroundings is very much like England, and game has been imported and the different societies and clubs have done much to acclimatize, breed and protect game. Here is a country where springer spaniels could

[124]

be more in evidence and worked with advantage. A good trade should spring up between New Zealand and California for gun dogs and greyhounds. The passage is one of less than three weeks, and the freight inconsiderate. All over South America gun dogs and greyhounds are required. There is some shooting in New Guinea, but the bush is very dense and the natives not always agreeable to the visitation of the man with a gun. Some very nice dogs are to be found in the Hawaiian Islands, notably at ever-glorious and salubrious Honolulu, the Paradise of the Pacific. And within a few days' hail is the Golden Gate and the ever-bountiful lands that slope down to the North Pacific and the longed-for port by the voyagers from the far East and the farther South. Here, of course, we will find gun dogs in great variety, and many greyhounds. Some years ago several of the best running dogs in England were imported by sportsmen in California. And that stock is in the Golden State now. Gun dogs are not only esteemed as gun dogs or for their looks, but also for their good looks. The English setter is bred in all his attractive loveliness and usefulness all the way up the Pacific Coast as far as British Columbia. And it is in the last mentioned province that some of the most beautiful of the blue-ticked, long and silver silk-like coated setting dogs have been bred. Taking the whole of the North American Continent we will find it one abiding place for gun dogs of the highest merit; and as it is well known, Americans and Canadians have always been circumspect and generous in their importations of gun dogs from Europe, and, consequently, have possessed themselves of specimens that are not only good to look upon, but easy to train and delightful to shoot over.

Whippet Dogs and Whippet Racing

THE whippet is a greyhound-like dog, and is the fastest of all dogs at his weight or height. In some instances they have been crossed with Italian greyhounds, but these alliances are apt to bring about inferior whippets for racing or catching rabbits, either on their own ground or at rabbit-coursing or snap-dog matches. In rabbit-coursing, where the rabbits have previously been caught and turned down on unknown ground (to the rabbit) before a brace of whippets, it is the dog *that catches* the rabbit that wins the course, and the winner of the majority of a given number of courses wins the wager for its owner or connections. Snap-dog coursing—that is, running rabbits down with whippets in small and enclosed places, the rabbit being given little "law," is not considered a sportsmanlike action, and is practiced only as a means of gambling. Whippets have long been declared a pure breed, and this dog was first recognized as such by the English Kennel Club.

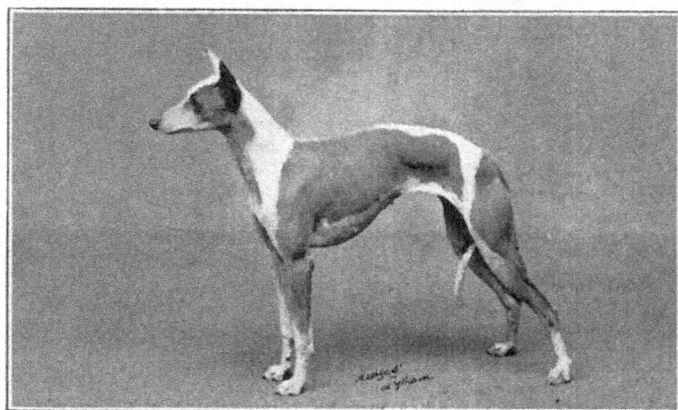

The Whippet

Whippet racing is an old sport and the pastime of working men in England. He has been called the poor man's race-horse, as indeed he is, the dog providing sport and a means of speculation for men of slender means. Whippet racing is carried on right through the year in the Northwest and North of England. Of late years it has become a great sport in London and its suburbs, the principal handicaps being run off every other Sunday forenoons at Walthamstow. Whippet racing was patronized by the late King Edward VII of England, at the Ranelagh Club grounds, London, and the leading "country club" of its kind in the United Kingdom. Whippet racing has long been a sport in Belgium, France and Germany. Dog racing was also introduced into South Africa during the end of the last century, and valuable handicaps are run off on the diamond and gold fields. Whippet racing was first favored in the United States by the English operatives in the cotton mills in New England, especially in Massachusetts. The sport has been well and continuously conducted at country clubs around Boston and Philadelphia, which has put the pastime on a society basis. There is no cruelty in whippet racing. The dog is held on his mark by the neck and root of tail, and, starting off at pistol fire, the object of his run of 200 yards or less being a towel held by the runner-up—usually someone he knows—who stands, holloas and waves the "rag," as it is called, 10 yards beyond the winning line or mark. The dogs are handicapped according to their weight or height. The latter is not a popular mode and it is the weight of a dog that is considered practically everywhere. Roughly, it can be reckoned that a dog of say 16 pounds is 2½ to 3 yards faster than a 15-pound dog. A bitch is keener than a dog. The handicap scale given in this description of the whippet was arranged by Freeman Lloyd and is largely in use throughout the world.

Finish in an Old-time Whippet Race Meeting

A whippet track may be easily laid out on grass, race track, show or fair ground. It must be 220 yards straight. If it is over, so much the better. The further the onlookers are kept off the track the more they can see, and they will not interfere with the dogs running. The whippets are entered, their names, weights, colors and owners being given. Each owner pays an entry fee for each dog and these fees are generally made a sweepstake and the purse divided between the first, second and third dogs in the final heat. The dogs must be weighed before they run and an allowance is made of 4 ounces or 8 ounces either way in their stated weight. The handicap is run off in heats, the number of dogs in each heat varying according to the entry and the duration of the racing. Heats may be run off like clockwork, one lot of dogs starting off as the others are finishing; or it may be delayed when the number of dogs is limited. If 40 dogs are entered and an afternoon's sport desired they can be run off in heats of four dogs each. There would be then 10 winners of heats to run off in the semi-finals, which could be either two heats of five each or, better still, three heats with two fours and one of three dogs. The two winners, or the three winners of the semi-finals, must be run off in the final. Taking the three semi-finals for choice, there would be run off altogether 14 races, which would occupy about two hours. The owner of the second may challenge the weight of the winner, immediately after the final is run. The dog is then allowed 6 ounces to the usual allowance made before the running of its first heat.

Here is a plan of a track. If possible, the dogs should run so that the sun shall not be in their faces.

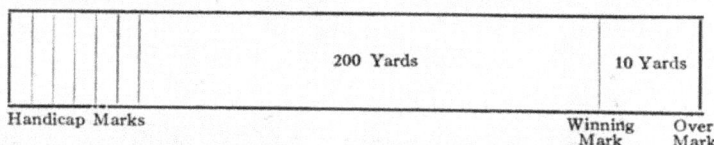

		200 Yards	10 Yards

Handicap Marks   Winning   Over
                                                          Mark   Mark

The dogs run in colors, strips of narrow ribbon being tied around their necks. These are of red, white, blue, yellow, green and black. On the race card the shade of the dog's racing color is noted in the preliminary heats. In the semi-final and final heats the back or scratch dog wears the red collar, the next the white, the next the blue, and so on. If the red dog is first over the winning line, where the judge stands, the judge raises a red flag. Whatever color wins so is a flag of the same color held aloft by the official whose ruling is final. Each "runner-up" must be behind the over or trig mark before his dog crosses the winning line. If dogs start when the cap is fired, but there is no powder explosion, it is no start. But if all dogs go fairly away, it is a start. Dead heats must be run off excepting in the final, where owners may agree to divide. If a dog is disqualified, the second dog takes his place in the records. No live bait allowed with the runner-up, and all dogs are subject to inspection by the officials. It is recommended that only whippets of 25 pounds or under be raced. The bigger dogs are often given to savaging or "slapping," and appear ungainly among a lot of small dogs. The back dog in every heat must run the whole of the 200 yards, or whatever smaller course is used.

STARTS FOR DOGS AND BITCHES OF DIFFERENT WEIGHTS IN 200 YARDS HANDICAP.

When a dog wins at a handicap he must be penalized according to the judgment of the handicapper. The following handicap would put each dog or bitch on equal terms, providing all the dogs were exactly of the same calibre or of equal racing powers—barring their weights:

Wt. of Dog or Bitch— Lbs.	Start for Dogs, Yd.	Start for Bitches, Yd.	Wt. of Dog or Bitch— Lbs.	Start for Dogs, Yd.	Start for Bitches, Yd.
28	1	0	16	16	13
27	2	1	15	18½	14½
26	3	2	14	21½	17
25	4	3	13	24½	20
24	5	4	12	27½	23½
23	6	5	11	31	26½
22	7	6	10	35	30
21	8	7	9	39	34
20	9½	7½	8	43	38
19	11	8	7	47	43
18	12½	9½	6	52	48
17	14	11	5	58	54

A dog covering 200 yards in 12 seconds gallops at the rate of 16 yards 24 inches a second; in 13 seconds, 15 yards 14 inches, and in 14 seconds, 14 yards 10 1-3 inches.

The Sled Dogs of Alaska

Between the laborer who earns his daily bread by the sweat of his brow, and the spoiled favorite of fortune who neither toils nor spins, there is not more difference than between the workers of the North—the Sled Dogs of Alaska—and the pampered, fur-coated, jewel-hung dogs "in society"; dogs who have their silk-lined baskets, their gold-mounted toilet articles, and the exclusive services of a personal attendant. But "Dogs is Dogs," and the unhappy accident of birth that gives to such a dog the humiliating experience of having his teeth brushed by a maid, or a massage of cold cream after a bath in a silver-plated tub, should not be held against him—for he may still retain some of his admirable, lovable canine qualities through the human veneer.

A dog's intelligence and his faithful, affectionate nature are his chief assets in his association with man; and if he preserves these in spite of his artificial surroundings as a mere toy, his development along those lines is almost unlimited when he becomes a co-worker with his master, and a devoted comrade through adversity and peril.

Far beyond the Aleutian Islands, which stretch a grim barrier between the North Pacific and Bering Sea, almost to the bleak coast of Siberia, there lies that part of Alaska not familiar to the average tourist. The Alaska of primeval forests, of great, almost unknown rivers, of vast areas of snow and ice that reach to the desolate shore of the Arctic—the Alaska of the Dogs; and here in the "Land that God forgot," the dog holds a unique place as an indispensable factor in the settlement of the country.

He discovered the North Pole with Peary; he discovered the South Pole and the Northwest Passage, too, with Amundsen; and he played a pathetic yet heroic part in the brave, if futile, efforts of Captain Scott to reach his goal; just as he has ever played well his role of support to those who have sought to penetrate the trackless wastes at the ends of the earth.

Late in October, usually under leaden skies, nearly the entire population of Nome stands upon a dreary beach watching the last boat of the open season, the "Victoria," steam slowly out through a sea already heavy with young ice, and disappear in the misty grayness of the horizon. The parting salute of the ship's siren has been answered by all of the town whistles; and then as if to add the fitting climax to the gloom of the occasion, it seems that every dog within hearing raises his voice to join in a mournful farewell chorus—a blood-curdling wail that is characteristic of these Northern dogs with their strong wolf strain.

But the people look with kindly eyes upon them, and even listen with kindly ears—for they know that every letter, paper, and magazine from now till the middle of June, will be brought in over fifteen hundred miles of ice and snow and frozen sea, by the United States Government Dog Team Mail; and that, except for the wireless system, all of the news from the great world "outside," from family and friends, depends upon

A Typical Scene in the Arctic Regions

Eskimo family and malamute—At Home.

these Postmen of the Silent Trails. They go where soft snow and other conditions make it impossible to use horses. No service is too lowly, no mission too high. They pull the baby in his tiny sled, are the means of delivery for the merchant, and they carry the doctor and priest to the bedside of the sick or dying in some lonely, distant cabin.

Owing to the prohibitive tax rate on railroads which traverse practically uninhabited districts in Seward Peninsula—a tax which has only been abolished within the past few months—dogs have become the motive power instead of engines; and in place of the "toot-toot" of the locomotive as it takes a freight train out to the mines with supplies, there is the "bow-wow" of the dog team "Kougarok Limited" or the "Little Creek Express" as it starts down the track with a loaded flat car.

As to "joy riding," the "Pupmobile" has every automobile completely outclassed when it comes to the maximum of joy, and the minimum of danger. Given a winter night when the frosty air brings the tingling blood to cheek and finger tip, when the glittering stars seem close above one's head in the clear sky, and when the trail glistens like a silver ribbon in the ghostly radiance of the Northern Lights, it is a phlegmatic person indeed who does not feel the thrill of excitement and delight that animates the dogs as they strain in their harness to be away for a spin across the snows.

Then there is the famous All Alaska Sweepstakes race each April from Nome on Bering Sea, to Candle on the Arctic Ocean and return, a distance of 408 miles; and the dogs as well as the men who have won their laurels in this contest are the sort of men and dogs who are making the History of Alaska—who are creating an Empire from a Wilderness.

There are two types of dogs used in the race. The Siberians, small, prick-eared, with bushy tails curled up over their backs, and with apparently decided traces of the fox; and the Alaskans who are of mixed breeds—setters, pointers, collies, hounds or what not—with a more or less pronounced wolf strain inherited from the McKenzie River Huskie or coast Malamute.

Both types have their staunch supporters, and for excellent reasons—for both possess wonderful qualities that endear them to dog users and dog lovers. The Siberians have not the speed, and many claim not the responsiveness and intelligence of the Alaskans—but they are gentle, tractable, easy to handle and are able to travel more steadily and with less rest than the others.

[129]

Dubby, a McKenzie River huskie, of the Allan and Darling Kennel, whose wonderful intelligence, and a record of over thirty thousand miles in harness, established his reputation as one of the greatest leaders Alaska has ever known.

The amount of rest in the race is a question of judgment with the driver, who must decide how much he can afford to take himself, and give his dogs without the unnecessary loss of a moment; but as he must return with every dog—dead or alive—with which he started, it is to his greatest advantage to keep them in the very best of condition. At every road-house and relay camp where they stop for food and sleep, it is "Dogs First," no driver thinking of himself till his team is fed, rubbed, and bedded. When they are tired or foot-sore, they ride in turn upon the sled, recuperating quickly in this way. Little moccasins of canton flannel are carried to be used on hard trails, and veils of black or green mosquito netting are placed over the dogs' eyes if the glare of the sun is too dazzling.

In the Sweepstakes of 1910, John Johnson, a Russian Finn, driving a team of Siberians entered by Colonel Charles Ramsay of London, came in first. The weather had been ideal, the trail perfect, and they had broken all records—covering the 408 miles in but little more than seventy-four hours. Closely following them was Charles Fox-Maule Ramsay, nephew of Colonel Ramsay, and younger brother of the Earl of Dalhousie, driving his own team of Siberians; and it certainly seemed that the day of the Siberians had come. But in 1911 and 1912, through terrible blizzards and over miserable trails, the Allan and Darling team of Alaskans, driven by "Scotty" Allan, were the winners; and in 1913, Fay Dalzene, with the Bowen-Dalzene dogs, was first, also using the Alaskan type. So that out of the seven great races that have been held under the auspices of the Nome Kennel Club since it was organized in 1908, five victories have fallen to the Alaskans, and the breaking of the record to the Siberians.

In short distances some of the dogs are remarkably fast, travelling at the rate of fifteen or sixteen miles an hour. Irish, one of the Allan and Darling team, a beautiful setter with some huskie blood, can pace a mile in three minutes; and Spot, a cross-bred

The starting of John Johnson's team of Siberians in one of the All Alaska Sweepstakes Races in Nome, Alaska.

pointer and huskie, after leading the team thirty miles over a heavy trail, covered four miles in thirteen minutes and twenty-five seconds without breaking.

As dog teams are not driven with reins, but by word of mouth, there must be in every team a particularly intelligent dog who is the leader. He must understand not only the simple orders "Mush" (go on), "Gee" (to the right), "Haw" (to the left), and "Stop," but he must have exceptionally quick instincts, a definite acknowledged mastery over the other dogs, and a sort of canine good judgment which tells him the right thing to do in difficulties and emergencies.

[131]

The stories of the marvellous sagacity of certain leaders are easy of belief to "the men that know the North" as Service calls them, but they would appear to be gross exaggerations or absolute untruths to those who have never seen dogs work in harness on the trail.

A leader has certain privileges, such as getting into the sled when the driver is not at the handle bars, and reposing in comfort and dignity on the furs while the rest of the dogs lie in the snow; and other perquisites which may occasion bitter jealousy and make necessary the utmost precaution in guarding him from the attacks of his envious team-mates. Sometimes an old leader, discarded or pensioned, will craftily wait for a chance to kill his successor—this chance generally occurring when the new aspirant for honors is tied and at a disadvantage. Some leaders, however, through wonderful strength and other superior qualities, become more or less exempt from this ill feeling, and their leadership is freely and pleasantly accepted both in and out of "business hours." Of these, Dubby, a magnificent specimen of the McKenzie River huskie, brought down from Dawson by "Scotty" Allan, was one of the most prominent. Dubby lived to be twelve years old, but was pensioned on his ninth birthday, while still in perfect condition and well able to enjoy the rewards of his faithful service. He had a record of over thirty thousand miles, in harness, to his credit, and the anecdotes of his intelligence are legion. He was often driven "loose," running ahead of the team instead of being hooked up with them; and he was so efficient as a "general manager" that the loss of his pulling power was of small moment compared to his ability to find and keep an obliterated trail, and his capacity for doing the many clever and helpful things that his active mind found to do. A mere hint that some dog was not working was enough, and Dubby would rush back to critically examine them all till the shirker was located by a slack tow line or traces not held taut. The culprit received a warning nip on the ear or flank, which was a threat of worse punishment if he did not mend his laggard habits; then Dub would dash off to give some other evidence of his real generalship. Perhaps it would be to decide that the ice on the river was not thick enough to bear the weight of the heavily loaded sled—for some strange instinct enabled him to know that fact, when an experienced Musher could be readily deceived; or he would choose the correct trail where many met and crossed, in spite of the efforts of an exasperated driver to convince him of the error of his ways. "You stubborn old Siwash (an insult indeed to apply the name of the most shiftless of Indians to a self-respecting huskie), I'll wager you're wrong; but do as you please, keep us all out here in thirty below weather, tired and hungry, and then maybe next time you'll listen to reason." But Dubby never did make the predicted mistake, and many a comfortable night's rest in shelter and warmth was the result of his unerring confidence in his own ability which no argument could disturb. He would politely wag his stump of a tail while he listened tolerantly to your opinion, but he ignored it with the same amiable disregard one would show toward the foolish suggestions of a babbling child.

The tragedies of the Arctic wastes are many, and would be more but for the faithful dogs; the list of canine heroes is long, and would be much longer were all of their brave deeds recorded. They have never, like some of whom we read, attended an "Acadamie pour Chiens," and acquired, with a diploma, such unnatural refinements and useless accomplishments as are displayed by "dogs in society." If invited to attend a luncheon of chicken à la Maryland, served on a decorated table, with Fifi and Bijou as fellow guests, they would not only demolish the chicken in short order, but also the decorations, and possibly Fifi and Bijou as well—classing them with cats and other legitimate prey.

There is no downy cushion before the blazing fire, no chosen corner of the limousine, no tooth brush or manicure set for the work dog of the North; yet they are probably happier than their kin of the governess and college education. They have no time for ennui—there are duties to be done, and it is rare indeed to find a sled dog who does not take pride in his task, show delight at the sight of his harness, and eagerly welcome the preparations for a good long mush.

Perhaps one of the most striking features of the races is the pleasure that the dogs manifest not only in the preliminary training, but in the contest itself. One frequently sees a team of dogs, old in the knowledge of racing, perfectly familiar with the hardships before them, waiting for the signal to leave, and so eager to be off, that three or four men are barely able to restrain them till the dip of the flag starts them on their dash to the Arctic. So, too, it is not unusual for a Mail Team, becoming impatient of the delay in unloading the mail, to run away after having carried a thousand pounds of mail for a distance of two or three hundred miles.

In summer when the dogs are not being used they often spend the time about mining camps where they are fed; or if in town they select one or more houses to which they make daily visits at meal hours if they find the inmates hospitably inclined. In many districts the dogs are virtually turned out to forage for themselves, when the wild strain in them asserts itself to an astonishing degree; but this is not true of Nome where dogs are held in high esteem, and where they are given the proper care at all seasons. And each year when the last boat of the summer sails from Nome, there is a long list of dog passengers. To a fancier they would seem undoubtedly a collection not worth their transportation; to my Lady of the Lap Dog they would cause shudders of disgust; there would be no place at the Bench Show for such as these. They are without pedigree, or beauty perhaps—mongrels if you will—but one never knows what a wealth of fidelity may be hidden beneath a rough exterior. Many a story that touches the heart may be extracted from the prospector going outside accompanied by some favorite dog who has shared his solitude and his hardships; who has helped to bear his burdens, and who is now to enjoy with him what they have earned together.

Perhaps that blind old huskie has guided his bewildered driver along the right trail to safety, true to the instincts of the wild, when the whirling snow and icy sleet cut like stinging whip lashes into the face and eyes, making sight impossible.

Perhaps this ragged, ungroomed malamute with his wolf head and his human heart, dragged himself with patient, bleeding feet, half starved and nearly frozen, to some remote camp with the warning that his unconscious master, caught unprepared in a sudden storm, needed help.

Perhaps—but after all, each tale is only another variation of the same theme: dog's loyalty to man. And as pampered pets, ôr as valued assistants, in society or out of it, this loyalty justifies the attention and regard they receive. It is the one thing all dogs have in common, and whether in their veins runs the blue blood of generations of prize winners, or the humble strain of some obscure street waif, it is to *You*, and not to what you possess, not for what you can offer him, that the dog gives his steadfast allegiance.

Sometimes when life has gone wrong with you
And the world seems a dreary place,
Has your dog ever silently crept to your feet,
His yearning eyes turned to your face—
Has he made you feel that he understands,
And all that he asks of you
Is to share your lot, be it good or ill,
With a chance to be loyal and true?
Are you branded a failure? He does not know—
A sinner? He does not care—
You're Master to him—that's all that counts—
A word, and his day is fair.
Your birth and your station are nothing to him;
A Palace and Hut are the same:
And his love is yours in honor and peace,
As it's yours through disaster and shame.
Though others forget you and pass you by,
He is ever your Faithful Friend,—
Ready to give you the best that is his,
Unselfishly, unto the End.

ESTHER BIRDSALL DARLING.

INDEX

"DOGS

OF ALL

NATIONS"

will give special displays on the

Panama-Pacific
International Exposition
Track and Polo Grounds

on SUNDAY afternoons and
other special occasions featuring
the following UTILITY DOGS:

SHEEP DOG TRIALS
POLICE DOG TRIALS
WAR DOG MANEUVERS
AMBULANCE DOG DRILL
ARCTIC SLED DOGS
WHIPPET RACING
PERFORMING DOGS
PARADE of the WORLD'S
CHAMPION BENCH DOGS

Dates and other information will be an-
nounced later.

Irish Wolfhound

Toyon
Southport St. Patrick

Farm raised puppies from
the best imported stock
usually For Sale.

TOYON KENNELS
LOS ALTOS, CALIFORNIA

[143]

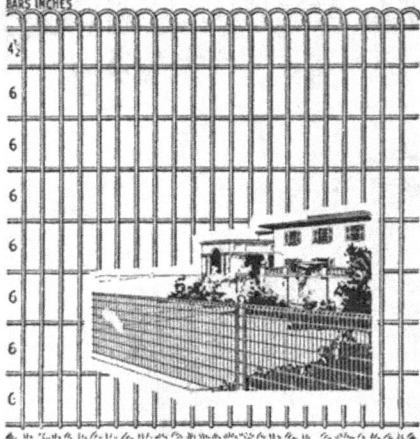

OTHER BOOKS BY VERTVOLTA PRESS